W9-CCD-110

My Name Is

OLD GLORY

A CELEBRATION OF THE STAR-SPANGLED BANNER

Martha LaGuardia-Kotite and Trish Marx

Foreword by Thad W. Allen, Admiral US Coast Guard (Ret.)

LP

LYONS PRESS
Guilford, Connecticut

An imprint of Globe Pequot Press

For all those who serve under the American flag,
and in memory of WWII veteran Charles J. LaGuardia, US Army,
and Ermin and Jean Windschill, who worked tirelessly
on the home front during the war

Text design: Eileen Hine
Project editor: Meredith Dias
Layout: Kirsten Livingston

Library of Congress Cataloging-in-Publication Data

LaGuardia-Kotite, Martha J.
My name is Old Glory : a celebration of the Star-Spangled Banner / Martha LaGuardia-Kotite and Trish Marx ; foreword by Thad W. Allen, Admiral US Coast Guard (Ret.).
 p. cm.
Includes poem "My Name is Old Glory," by Howard Schnauber.
ISBN 978-0-7627-7906-2
1. Flags—United States—History. I. Marx, Trish. II. Title.
CR113.L25 2012
929.9'20973—dc23
2011046300

Printed in the United States of America

10 9 8 7 6 5 4 3 2 1

Contents

Foreword by Thad W. Allen, Admiral US Coast Guard (Ret.) v

Introduction vi

"My Name Is Old Glory" by Howard Schnauber 1

O Say Can You See 56

"The Star-Spangled Banner" by Francis Scott Key 57

Flagmaker Mary Pickersgill 58

The Grand Union Flag 59

The Bennington Flag 60

The Restoration of the Original Star-Spangled Banner 61

Don't Tread on Me 63

The Flag Acts of 1777, 1794, and 1818 64

Memorial Day 68

Fleet Week 69

Flag Day 69

The Fourth of July 71

Armed Forces Day 72

Veterans Day 73

The Blue Angels 74

The Thunderbirds 75

The War of 1812 76

Revenue Cutters 76

The American Civil War, 1861–1865 77

World War I, 1914–1918 79

World War II, 1939–1945 81

Korean War, 1950–1953 83

Vietnam War, 1964–1973 84

The War on Terror, 2001–Present 86

Joplin, Missouri, May 22, 2011 87

Haiti, January 12, 2010 89

Hurricane Katrina, August 29, 2005 91

The Bering Sea Patrol 92

US Navy Divers 94

Washington's Crossing: The Story behind the Art 96

The Iwo Jima Memorial 100

The American Flag, Baseball, and the National Anthem 101

George Rodrigue's *God Bless America* 102

The National 9/11 Flag 105

The Pledge of Allegiance 107

Honoring the Flag 109

Displaying the Flag 111

Folding the Flag 113

Honoring Those Who Served 115

Tomb of the Unknowns 116

Bibliography 118

About the Authors 120

Foreword

Each day, in every country where our United States forces are stationed—in places like Afghanistan, Germany, Japan, and Korea—we hold ceremonies to recognize extraordinary service, bravery, and valor. We also honor those who are retiring after having faithfully and honorably served their country by presenting them with an American flag in appreciation for their commitment. These ceremonies become personal. In May 2010, when I was relieved as the Commandant of the Coast Guard, I was presented a folded flag by the Master Chief Petty Officer of the Coast Guard. Together we walked from the podium down to the front row, where my father was seated. There I presented my flag to Chief Damage Controlman, USCG (Ret.) Bill Allen, a World War II veteran and member of the Greatest Generation.

By exercising the manners of our profession, we reaffirm our core values and say to new generations, "This is what is important." Many times these ceremonies include the recitation of the poem "My Name Is Old Glory." The images evoked by these stirring words bind the speaker and those in attendance in a common understanding that we, as United States citizens, are part of something larger than ourselves. It gives us pause to reflect, to celebrate, to honor our past and look with optimism to the future. In this book, Martha LaGuardia-Kotite and Trish Marx have captured with stunning imagery each word, each phrase of this poem attributed to Howard Schnauber. While there may be many coffee-table books displayed in our homes, few carry the meaning and significance of this book. My thanks to Martha, Trish, and their team for bringing the words of "My Name Is Old Glory" visually to life. It is a gift that will be cherished now and well into the future.

—**Admiral Thad W. Allen,**
US Coast Guard (Ret.)
October 2011

Introduction

The first time I heard the poem "My Name Is Old Glory," I could barely hold back my emotion. The powerful verse was read aloud at a military retirement ceremony while the folded flag was ceremoniously presented to the honored veteran. The words had a striking effect on everyone in the audience. After witnessing this reaction, I was determined to find out who wrote this mighty tribute to our flag.

I learned that the poem was attributed to US Marine Corps enlisted man Howard Schnauber. Orphaned at an early age, Schnauber joined the Civilian Conservation Corps and then signed on with the Marines. He fought in both World War II and the Korean War and earned four Purple Hearts. After his return from World War II, Schnauber became an active supporter of veterans' needs. Perhaps his favorite pastime, however, was teaching children to appreciate and respect the flag.

My friend and co-author, Trish Marx, joined me in creating a tribute to this poem and the American flag. We are pleased and honored to share the power and presence of "My Name Is Old Glory" with you. The American flag is an expression of what unites us as Americans.

"My Name Is Old Glory" celebrates the spirit of the United States of America and the true love Americans have for their

Howard Schnauber, US Marine Corps.
(Courtesy of the Fort Collins Local History Archive and Howard Schnauber, 1994)

Judith Downey holds the flag that was presented to her husband, Master Chief Petty Officer John Downey, and listens to him speak about his forty-one years of Coast Guard service during his retirement ceremony on June 20, 2008, at Station Point Judith in Narragansett, Rhode Island. Downey was the first Ancient Keeper, an honor that recognizes outstanding performance and longevity of service in Coast Guard boat forces operations. He had held the title for five years before passing it on to Chief Warrant Officer Kevin Galvin during the ceremony. *(Coast Guard photo by Petty Officer Second Class Lauren Jorgensen)*

country. This book highlights historical events that unfolded from the War of 1812, when "The Star-Spangled Banner" was written, to the present day with moving and inspiring photographs that celebrate our flag, our people, and our nation.

This story explores today's military, the world of first responders, and the ways towns and cities across America celebrate with Old Glory—at football and baseball games, in art and in classrooms, and with monuments honoring those who have served. Included are some of the tragic moments in our history, when Americans needed the strength and unity of patriotism the most. This is the story of how our flag has waved tall and proud while becoming a true testament of our country's values.

Where there is this spirit, there flies the American flag. In times of joy, we have seen the flag wave proudly above the fifty-yard line or in the hand of a small child during a Fourth of July celebration. In times of war, we have witnessed the flag sail into harbors on the masts of our ships or lead troops into conflicts around the world and later bring them home.

The story of our flag, our people, and our nation is never finished—nor is the power of the enduring American spirit embodied by Old Glory.

We are donating a portion of the proceeds from the sale of this book to help veterans. Thank you for your support!

MY NAME IS OLD GLORY
by HOWARD SCHNAUBER

I am the flag of the United States of America.

This image of *Washington Crossing the Delaware* depicts Gen. George Washington leading his men across the Delaware River on a frigid Christmas night in 1776 during the Revolutionary War. Once on the other side, Washington and his troops surprised the slumbering Hessian troops in Trenton, defeating them in minutes. The original painting is twelve feet high and twenty-one feet long. In his work, the artist, Emanuel Leutze, evokes the courage of the moment. *(Photo credit: Art Resource, NY ART39923)*

My name is Old Glory.

A parachutist drifts to the ground with the American flag during the opening ceremony for the Gathering of Mustangs and Legends, an air show featuring P-51 Mustangs flown in World War II and the heroes who flew them, at Rickenbacker International Airport in Columbus, Ohio.

(US Air Force photo by Senior Airman Amanda Cain)

I fly atop the world's tallest buildings.

New York City. *(Photo by Trish Marx)*

I stand watch in America's halls of justice.

Along Pennsylvania Avenue in Washington, D.C., the Constitution, the Bill of Rights, and the Declaration of Independence are displayed in the Rotunda of the National Archives Building. *(Photo by Martha LaGuardia-Kotite)*

I fly majestically over great institutes of learning.

Flags fly with equal grandeur over one-room schoolhouses and on large campuses, such as this one at Columbia University in New York City. *(Photo by Trish Marx)*

I stand guard with the greatest military power in the world.

USS *Nimitz* (CVN-68) steams alongside the USS *Princeton* as the American flag waves proudly in the wind. *Princeton* was part of the *Nimitz* battle group exercising off the California coast in 2002. *(Photo credit: US Navy)*

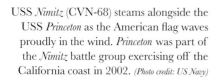

Look up!—and see me!

Signalman Third Class Christopher Clark raises the American flag on the signal bridge aboard USS *George Washington* (CVN-73), during Operation Iraqi Freedom in 2004. *(US Navy photo by Michael D. Blackwell II)*

I stand for peace—honor—truth and justice.

Participants, some carrying American flags, join together in the civil rights march from Selma to Montgomery, Alabama, in 1965. *(Photo credit: Peter Pettus, Library of Congress Exhibit Voices of Civil Rights)*

I stand for freedom.

John Roebling, an immigrant from Germany, dreamed of spanning the East River and designed the Brooklyn Bridge, which holds the American flag for anyone who takes the breathtaking walk across this beautiful landmark to see. *(Photo credit: Todd Vorenkamp, www.trvphoto.com)*

I am confident—   I am arrogant.   I am proud.

The son of a sailor assigned aboard the guided missile destroyer USS *O'Kane* (DDG-77) waves an American flag as the ship returns to Pearl Harbor, Hawaii, from a six-month deployment. *(US Navy photo by Journalist Third Class Ryan C. McGinley)*

A USCG motor lifeboat from Coast Guard Station Humboldt Bay powers through the entrance to Humboldt Bay, California. *(Photo credit: Todd Vorenkamp, www.trvphoto.com)*

Ali Matos, three, celebrates July Fourth in New York City. *(Photo credit: Ydania Matos)*

When I am flown with my fellow banners, my head is a little higher,

Bluewater Elementary School in Niceville, Florida, flies the American flag and the Florida state flag. *(Photo by Amy Moye)*

My colors a little truer.

Air Force Academy cadets keep a giant American flag aloft during the Air Force–Brigham Young University 9/11 memorial ceremony at Falcon Stadium near Colorado Springs, Colorado, in 2010. The flag measured about fifty-five yards by thirty yards. *(US Air Force photo by Dennis Rogers)*

I bow to no one.

Torn but resolute, an American flag lies in
the rubble of the World Trade Center after
the September 11, 2001, terrorist attacks.

(US Navy photo by Preston Keres)

I am recognized all over the world.

A Chilean honor guard member holds both the American and the Chilean flags during a ceremony at the Monument to the Heroes of Iquique during Southern Partnership Station 2011, which is an annual deployment of US ships to the US Southern Command area of responsibility in the Caribbean and Latin America. *(US Navy photo by Mass Communication Specialist Second Class Ricardo J. Reyes / Released)*

Boy, Girl, and Cub Scouts partake in a flag ceremony during an assembly at A. T. Mahan Elementary School at Naval Air Station Keflavik, Iceland. The American flag used in the ceremony was raised and lowered over the Pentagon on August 30, 2002, in honor of those who died during the terrorist attack on September 11, 2001. *(US Navy photo by Art Frith)*

Spc. Samantha Romero, a medic assigned to Headquarters and Headquarters Company, First Brigade Combat Team, Fourth Infantry Division, shows Rafi his new Chemlite mobile, handmade by medics at the Camp Nathan Smith Medical Aid Station in Afghanistan, September, 15, 2010. Rafi, a six-month-old Afghan boy, was admitted for complications related to a rare congenital heart defect. *(US Army photo by Spc. Breanne Pye)*

Peruvians waiting in line for medical care in Salaverry, Peru, in August 2007 display an American flag. Medical personnel attached to the Military Sealift Command (MSC) hospital ship USNS *Comfort* were at the school providing dental, optometric, pediatric, and adult medicine services. *Comfort* was on a four-month humanitarian deployment to Latin America and the Caribbean. *(US Navy photo by Elizabeth R. Allen)*

I am worshipped—I am saluted—I am respected

Adm. (Ret.) Thad W. Allen, then Commandant of the Coast Guard, salutes the national ensign—or national flag flown on a ship—during the Coast Guard District Thirteen change of command ceremony. Allen presided over the ceremony as Rear Adm. John P. Currier relieved Rear Adm. Richard R. Houck, who retired from the Coast Guard after thirty-two years of service. *(Official Coast Guard photo by Petty Officer Third Class David Marin)*

I am revered—

US Marines with C Company, Battalion Landing Team 1/1 of the Fifteenth Marine Expeditionary Unit, Special Operations Capable (MEU, SOC), raised the first American flag in Afghanistan in November 2001, as Operation Swift Freedom began. *(Photo credit: USMC Sgt. Joseph R. Chenelly)*

I am loved,

Naval Station Great Lakes sailors unfurl a giant American flag (150 feet by 300 feet) before the Chicago White Sox face the Cleveland Indians at US Cellular Field in Chicago, on April 4, 2005. *(US Navy photo by Elijah Leinaar)*

and I am feared.

The F-22's aeronautical design and flight controls allow it to outmaneuver its adversaries.

(Photo credit: US Air Force Tech. Sgt. Justin D. Pule)

I have fought every battle of every war for more than 200 years

The Dignity Memorial Vietnam Wall, a traveling three-quarter-scale replica of the Washington, D.C., memorial, is photographed in San Diego, California. It stands 240 feet long and 8 feet high. The wall lists the names of more than fifty-eight thousand fallen heroes of the Vietnam War. *(US Navy Photographer's Mate First Class Marvin Harris)*

Gettysburg, Shiloh, Appomattox, San Juan Hill, the trenches of France, the Argonne Forest, Anzio, Rome, the beaches of Normandy, the deserts of Africa,

Spc. Jacob Johns yells for another 155 mm round as Sgt. Nathan Hughes lines up a target during a retirement ceremony for the M198 howitzer at Camp Atterbury Joint Maneuver Training Center, Indiana, on September 18, 2010. Both soldiers are cannon crew members assigned to the Second Battalion, 150th Artillery Regiment. *(US Army photo by Sgt. Will Hill)*

the cane fields of the Philippines, the rice paddies and jungles of Guam, Okinawa, Japan, Korea, Vietnam, Guadalcanal, New Britain, Peleliu, and many more islands.

Chow is served to American infantrymen in the 347th Infantry Regiment on their way to La Roche, Belgium, in January 1945 during World War II. *(Photo credit: National Archives 113 photo no. 111-SC-198849)*

And a score of places long forgotten

In 1944, two Coast Guard–manned landing ship tanks (LSTs) open their great jaws in the surf that washes on Leyte Island beach, as soldiers strip down and build sandbag piers out to the ramps to speed up unloading operations. *(Photo credit: National Archives 151 photo no. 26-G-3738)*

by all but those who were with me.

American prisoners of war celebrate July 4, 1942, in the Japanese prison camp of Casisange in Malaybalay, on Mindanao, Philippines. It was against Japanese regulations, and discovery would have meant death, but the men celebrated the occasion anyway. *(Photo credit: National Archives 172 photo no. 111-SC-333290)*

I was there.

The motion of its props causes an aura to form around this F6F Hellcat on USS *Yorktown*. Rotating with blades, the halo moves aft, giving depth and perspective. November 1943. *(Photo credit: National Archives 70 photo no. 80-G-204747A)*

I led my soldiers—

Pilots deployed to fight the war on terrorism take American flags on missions for family and friends.
(US Air Force photo by D. Myles Cullen)

I followed them.

Marines from Marine Barracks Washington participate in the 2009 presidential inaugural parade in downtown Washington, D.C. *(Photo credit: US Navy)*

I watched over them.

Coast Guardsmen Casey Hanchette (foreground), a rescue swimmer, and David Ashey, an aviation maintenance technician, scan flooded areas of Cameron, Louisiana, for anyone needing assistance during an overflight on September 13, 2008, following Hurricane Ike's landfall. *(USCG photo by Thomas M. Blue)*

They loved me.

Navy slotback Tony Lane (21) and linebacker Ben Matthews (50) lead the US Naval Academy football team onto the field prior to the 104th Army-Navy game in Philadelphia, Pennsylvania.

(US Navy photo by Damon J. Moritz)

I was on a small hill in Iwo Jima.

The famous sculpture of five Marines and a Navy corpsman raising an American flag atop Mount Suribachi commemorates the 6,800 service members who died capturing the Japanese island of Iwo Jima during World War II. *(US Navy photo by Kevin S. O'Brien)*

I was dirty,

A US Coast Guard member of the Atlantic Strike Team helps to monitor the air quality and coordinate equipment and personnel wash-downs amid the rubble of the World Trade Center in New York City following the 9/11 attack. *(Photo credit: US Coast Guard William Barry)*

battle-worn and tired,

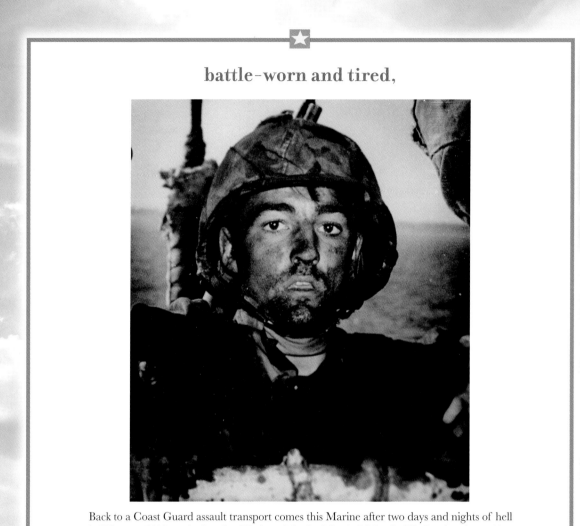

Back to a Coast Guard assault transport comes this Marine after two days and nights of hell in February 1944 on the beach of Eniwetok in the Marshall Islands. His face is grimy with coral dust, but the light of battle stays in his eyes. *(Photo credit: National Archives 146 photo no. 26-G-3394)*

but my soldiers cheered me,

Waving flags of the United States, Great Britain, and Holland, gaunt Allied prisoners of war at Aomori camp near Yokohama, Japan, cheer rescuers from the US Navy, August 29, 1945. *(Photo credit: National Archives 176 photo no. 80-G-490444)*

and I was proud.

Soldiers show respect to a fallen comrade
returning home in a flag-draped coffin.

(Photo credit: US Air Force S.Sgt. Joseph McKee)

I have been soiled, burned, torn and trampled on the streets of countries I have helped set free.

Burning a country's flag is a form of extreme protest. Congressional laws passed over the years banning flag-burning in the United States have been struck down by the Supreme Court on the grounds that they inhibit free speech. Only a constitutional amendment can give states the right to pass laws prohibiting American flag desecration. *(Photo by Trish Marx)*

It does not hurt, for I am invincible.

Thunderbirds in formation above Edwards Air Force Base, California, 2006.

(Photo credit: US Air Force)

I have been soiled, burned, torn and trampled on the streets of my country, and when it is by those with whom I have served in battle—it hurts.

Soldiers and sailors tear up a flag carried by Socialists during a peace demonstration in Boston.

(Photo credit: National Archives 123 photo no. 165-WW-158A-4)

But I shall overcome—for I am strong.

American photographer Thomas E. Franklin's famous image depicts firefighters raising the American flag at the World Trade Center after the September 11, 2001, terrorist attack on New York. Pictured here are Daniel McWilliams (center), William Eisengrein (right), and George Johnson. This image has raised more than $10 million to help families and rescue workers of 9/11. *(Used with permission. Photo copyright: 2001 The* Record, *Bergen County, New Jersey, photo by Thomas E. Franklin)*

I have slipped the bonds of Earth

The American flag heralds the flight of Apollo 11, the first lunar landing mission. The Apollo 11 Saturn V space vehicle lifted off with astronauts Neil A. Armstrong, Michael Collins, and Edwin E. "Buzz" Aldrin Jr. at 9:32 a.m. (EDT) on July 16, 1969, from Kennedy Space Center's Launch Complex 39A. *(Photo credit: NASA)*

and stand watch over the uncharted new frontiers of space

Moonset over the Earth limb taken on July 14, 1995, from space shuttle *Discovery* during STS-70 mission. *(Photo credit: NASA)*

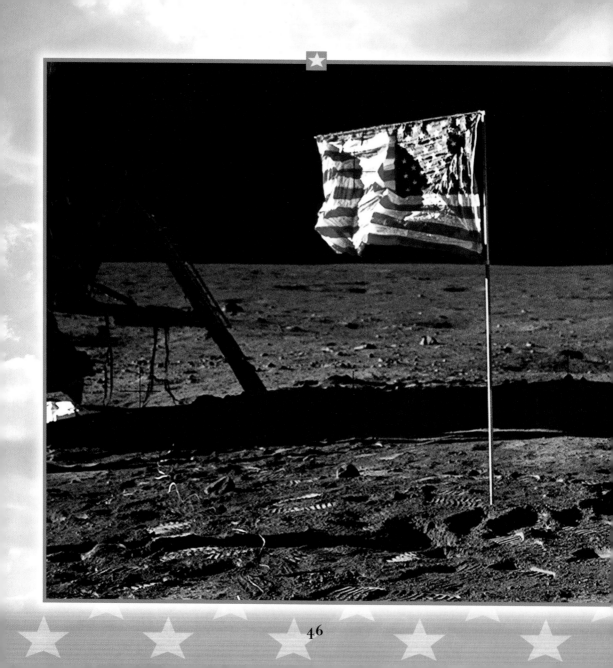

from my vantage point on the moon.

Astronaut Buzz Aldrin, lunar module pilot of the first lunar landing mission, poses for a photograph beside the deployed United States flag during an Apollo 11 extravehicular activity (EVA) on the lunar surface. *(Photo credit: NASA)*

I have been a silent witness to all of America's finest hours.

(Photo credit: Northwest Florida Daily News, *Nick Tomecek)*

But my finest hour comes when I am torn into strips to be used for bandages for my wounded comrades on the field of battle,

During an average month in 2007, hundreds of wounded soldiers passed under the American flag–emblazoned canopy known as Hero's Highway at the Air Force Theater Hospital at Balad Air Base, Iraq. *(Photo credit: US Air Force Tech. Sgt. Cecillio M. Ricardo Jr., Hero's Highway, Iraq)*

When I fly at half-mast to honor my soldiers,

Honored guests fill the USS *Memorial* while the national ensign flies at half-mast during a ceremony to commemorate the sixty-first anniversary of the December 7, 1941, attack on Pearl Harbor. *(Photo credit: US Navy Photographer's Mate Airman Benjamin D. Glass)*

Survivors of the December 7, 1941, Japanese attack on Pearl Harbor salute as the US Pacific Command Joint Services Color Guard presents the colors during a ceremony commemorating the sixty-ninth anniversary of the attack. About two hundred survivors and three thousand members of the public attended the ceremony. *(US Navy photo by Mass Communication Specialist Second Class Michael Russell/Released)*

and when I lie in the trembling arms of a grieving mother at the graveside of her fallen son.

Famed Doolittle Raider US Air Force M.Sgt. (Ret.) Ed Horton Jr., a World War II hero, passed away in Fort Walton Beach, Florida, and was given full military honors at his funeral service.

(Photo credit: Nick Tomecek, Northwest Florida Daily News)

I am proud.

US Coast Guard Cutter *Eagle* under full sail in San Francisco Bay. Coast Guard Academy cadets and officer candidates gain unparalleled leadership and seamanship experience at sea aboard America's Tall Ship. *(Photo credit: Bruce Bennett, USCG Auxiliary)*

My name is Old Glory.
Dear God—
Long may I wave.

Within a counter-IED compound,
an American flag flies at sunrise in
Afghanistan. *(Photo credit: Brad Kline)*

O Say Can You See

On September 13, 1814, a British fleet of nineteen ships unleashed a twenty-five-hour bombardment on Fort McHenry in Baltimore Harbor during the War of 1812. When the fighting started, Francis Scott Key, a thirty-four-year-old lawyer, was on a nearby British ship, arranging for the successful release of a prisoner. Key stayed up all night, pacing the ship's deck, staring into the blackness and fog. He could see little, but he could hear the guns thundering. *Whose guns?* he thought. *Which side is winning?*

In the first rays of dawn, he saw the huge American flag flying above the fort, which had not surrendered. Key took a letter from his pocket and began to write his thoughts on the back of it. He had in mind the melody to a British tune as he scribbled down words to fit. Key revised the verse when he returned to shore, first naming and publishing it as "The Defence of Fort McHenry." Later the popular piece was renamed "The Star-Spangled Banner." According to *Our Flag*, published by the US Congress, Key said years later, "I saw the flag of my country waving over a city—the strength and pride of my native State—a city devoted to plunder and desolation by its assailants. I witnessed the preparation for its assaults. I saw the array of its enemies as they advanced to the attack. I heard the sound of battle; the noise of the conflict fell upon my listening ear, and told me that 'the brave and the free' had met the invaders." In 1931 the song became our national anthem.

Original manuscript of "The Star-Spangled Banner," 1814. Title from unverified caption data received with the Harris & Ewing Collection Gift, 1955. *(Photo credit: Library of Congress)*

> *"While we routinely hear the song played at ceremonies and sporting events, the true motivational power and meaning that caused Francis Scott Key to put pen to paper in 'The Star-Spangled Banner' as he witnessed the valiant defense of Fort McHenry in the Battle of Baltimore, September 13–14, 1814, is actually more truly reflected by reading the text of that old 'bar room ballad.' So my reflection is to take pause and reflect on these words and how Old Glory inspired one man and lives on to inspire us all."* —**Scot S. Graham, New York**

THE STAR-SPANGLED BANNER
by Francis Scott Key, September 1814
(Sung to the tune of "To Anacreon in Heaven")

O say! can you see, by the dawn's early light,
What so proudly we hail'd at the twilight's last gleaming?
Whose broad stripes and bright stars, thro' the perilous fight,
O'er the ramparts we watched were so gallantly streaming?
And the rockets' red glare, the bombs bursting in air,
gave proof thro' the night that our flag was still there.
O say! does that Star-Spangled Banner yet wave
O'er the land of the free and the home of the brave?

On the shore, dimly seen thro' the mist of the deep,
Where the foe's haughty host in dread silence reposes,
What is that which the breeze, o'er the towering steep,
As it fitfully blows, half conceals, half discloses?
Now it catches the gleam of the morning's first beam,
In full glory reflected now shines in the stream.
'Tis the Star-Spangled Banner. O long may it wave
O'er the land of the free and the home of the brave.

And where is that band who so vauntingly swore,
That the havoc of war and the battle's confusion
A home and a country should leave us no more?
Their blood has wash'd out their foul footstep's pollution.
No refuge could save the hireling and slave
From the terror of flight or the gloom of the grave,
And the Star-Spangled Banner in triumph doth wave
O'er the land of the free and the home of the brave.

O thus be it ever when freemen shall stand
Between their lov'd home and war's desolation,
Blest with vict'ry and peace, may the Heav'n-rescued land
Praise the pow'r that hath made and preserv'd us a nation.
Then conquer we must, when our cause it is just,
And this be our motto, "In God is our trust."
And the Star-Spangled Banner in triumph shall wave
O'er the land of the free and the home of the brave.

> *"Seeing the flag, much like singing 'The Star-Spangled Banner,' gives me pause. I reflect. I appreciate my country and pause to remember its symbolic colors of freedom."* —**Diane Mitchell, Florida**

Flagmaker Mary Pickersgill

One of Major George Armistead's first orders of business when he took command of Fort McHenry during the War of 1812 was to find the best flagmaker in Baltimore, Maryland. He wanted Fort McHenry to fly a flag so big that it could be seen from great distances.

Second-grade students at Bluewater Elementary School in Niceville, Florida, perform a skit about Betsy Ross and other helpers making the flag.

(Photo by Robyn Bomar)

His search soon led to respected flagmaker Mary Pickersgill, who purchased four hundred yards of first-quality handwoven wool bunting, dyed red for the stripes and blue for the star field, and quantities of white cotton for the stars. She set to work along with four other women—her daughter, two of her nieces, and an indentured servant—making two flags for Major Armistead. The first, known as a storm flag, was seventeen by twenty-five feet, close to the standard size used today at forts. The second, though, was much larger, at thirty by forty-two feet. Its stripes were two feet wide, and its stars measured two feet across. As a good flagmaker would, Mary reinforced the topping, or heading, of the flag.

Toward dawn on September 14, 1814, after a hard-fought battle at Fort McHenry, Major Armistead ordered the smaller flag to be taken down and the large garrison flag to be raised. Through the mist and smoke, the flag that became known as the Star-Spangled Banner could be seen for miles. Baltimore was successfully defended, and it was a turning point in the war. The flag was flying proud, and the nation was saved.

The Grand Union Flag

Tradition has it that our first national flag was flown on January 1, 1776, when George Washington ordered that a "Union flag in compliment to [the] united colonies" be raised on a seventy-six-foot flagstaff in Cambridge, Massachusetts, to celebrate the day the Continental Army was formally brought into existence. Washington used the Meteor Flag of Great Britain. He kept the pattern of St. George's and St. Andrew's Crosses on the upper left corner but added thirteen white stripes on the large red field and renamed it the Grand Union Flag. By keeping the original cross design on the flag, he was indicating an affiliation with Great Britain. British soldiers believed it a declaration of allegiance to Great Britain, but to the colonists, it was a powerful symbol of their desire for independence. By the summer of 1776, this flag was obsolete. The Declaration of Independence had been signed, and it was no longer possible to reconcile with the mother country. The colonists were now revolutionaries, fighting for their independence. In a letter to his military secretary, Col. Joseph Reed, on January 4, 1776, Washington wrote, ". . . for on that day, the day which gave being to a new army, but before the proclamation [a speech from King George III] came to hand, we had hoisted the Union flag in compliment to the United Colonies."

> *"The American flag is a symbol of freedom and love. It is a symbol of how America was formed. It shows the events that happened in American history. Last but not least, I believe that it symbolizes the courageous soldiers who fought for our country."* **—Amethyst Simmons, age eleven**

The Bennington Flag

For many years, it was believed that the Bennington Flag was flown at the Battle of Bennington on August 16, 1777, making it the oldest Stars and Stripes flag in existence. According to tradition, Nathaniel Fillmore, grandfather of Millard Fillmore, the thirteenth US president from 1850 to 1853, raised the flag, which was the first one raised in victory in the Revolutionary War.

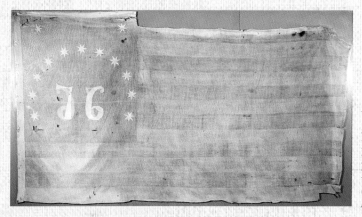

You can see the flag at the Bennington Battle Monument and Historical Association in Bennington, Vermont.
(Photo credit: Bennington Museum, Bennington, Vermont)

This is a lovely story, but, alas, modern technology tells another story. The fabric is not linen, but instead is cotton spun on a machine in a way that was not used before 1800. However, it's still an old flag—dating from 1800 to 1820. And it's still magnificent to see because it embodies an important part of our country's history.

The Restoration of the Original Star-Spangled Banner

The National Museum of American History, part of the Smithsonian Institution in Washington, D.C., reopened in 2008 after a two-year, $85 million renovation. The centerpiece of the museum is—you guessed it—the original Star-Spangled Banner, the very one that Francis Scott Key saw "in the dawn's early light."

The flag was removed from the museum's walls in 1994 after years of public viewing. The museum directors called in fifty conservators, flag historians, scientists, and curators, who put their heads together and developed a plan. There would be a complete restoration and a new home for our national treasure.

To give you an idea of the flag's size, it had to be housed in a forty-by-fifty-foot environmentally controlled laboratory during restoration. Chief conservator for the project Suzanne Thomassen-Krauss said that flags have a hard life and that this flag would never fly again. But it would be restored and put on view permanently, grandly declaring its place in our country's history. Here's what it took to preserve and conserve the Star-Spangled Banner according to the museum:

- ten months of painstaking removal of 1.7 million stitches attaching it to the linen backing
- more painstaking removal of sixty repairs and previous mendings that stressed the delicate fabric

- a cleaning of the 1,020 square feet of material with cosmetic sponges as workers lay on their stomachs on a platform inches above the flag

- a second cleaning, and then sewing of the fabric to a support material

- the attaching of a laminate used in sailboat sails to the back of the flag

- the construction of a temperature-, light-, humidity-, and oxygen-controlled exhibit hall

The original Star-Spangled Banner. *(Photo credit: Armed Forces History Division, National Museum of American History, Smithsonian Institution)*

Finally, after eight years, the Star-Spangled Banner, in all its glory, was back on display. It is resting, says Thomassen-Krauss, but accessible to anyone who wants to see it.

Thank you, Smithsonian. And thank you to Ralph Lauren, who donated the funds to restore the original Star-Spangled Banner.

"The American flag for me represents a dream that is America. It represents the grit and raw determination of those who first settled this vast country, and the sacrifices and unimaginable courage of soldiers who came before me and fought in our nation's wars. The flag represents the struggling single mothers who work two jobs and do what is needed to feed their children. It also represents the men and women who spent twenty years working a seventy-hour week at manufacturing jobs that got outsourced to a foreign country for higher corporate profits. The flag represents all that is America. It is flawed glory, but it still makes me proud!" —**S.Sgt. Daniel Jay Cooper, 519th Military Police Battalion, United States Army**

Don't Tread on Me

During the early years of the American Revolution, there was no standard American flag. People were free to make their own flags, and many did—some out of nothing more than rags. Flags could be any color, with any design on them, but they all were intensely symbolic. In the southern colonies in particular, the rattlesnake became a powerful symbol. This is attributed partly to Benjamin Franklin, who wrote in a 1751 satire that the colonies should send rattlesnakes to Britain just as the British had sent convicts to America.

In 1775, Col. Christopher Gadsden of South Carolina presented the Continental Congress with a rattlesnake flag carrying the words "Don't Tread on Me." It was used on naval ships and was first raised on the *Alfred*, helmed by the commander in chief of the Navy. Later, a flag named the First Navy Jack placed the snake and the words against a background of thirteen red and white stripes.

The Gadsden Flag. *(Credit: flagline.com)*

The First Navy Jack. *(Credit: flagline.com)*

Why has the rattlesnake been used again and again to symbolize the colonies? Scholars believe Franklin wrote to the *Pennsylvania Journal* in December 1775 that the rattlesnake, with its sharp eyes, "may therefore be esteemed an emblem of vigilance. . . . She never begins an attack, nor, when once engaged, ever surrenders. She is therefore an emblem of magnanimity and true courage. . . . She never wounds 'til she has generously given notice, even to her enemy, and cautioned him against the danger of treading on her." In 2002, in response to the 9/11 terrorist attacks, the secretary of the Navy directed all Navy ships to fly the First Navy Jack on the jackstaff (a small pole on the bow of a ship on which a flag called the "jack" is flown) under the flag of the United States Navy. Most ships added the rattlesnake flag on September 11, 2002, and will fly it until the war on terrorism is over.

The Flag Acts of 1777, 1794, and 1818

The new nation, after declaring its independence in 1776, was still fighting a long, desperate struggle against a formidable enemy. Its flags were homegrown and often symbolic of a region. The new nation needed a uniform flag to continue the momentum of independence and unify the values that formed it. To that end, on June 14, 1777, the Continental Congress passed the first Flag Act: "Resolved, That the flag of the United States be made of thirteen stripes alternate red and white, that the union be thirteen stars, white in a blue field, representing a new Constellation." The placement of the stars and the proportions of the stripes were left up to the individual flagmaker, however, so there is an interesting variety of flags from this period.

After Vermont, in 1791, and Kentucky, in 1792, were admitted to the Union, Congress passed the Second Flag Act in 1794, stating that by May 1795 the flag would have fifteen stripes and fifteen stars. The Star-Spangled Banner that flew over Fort McHenry in 1814 is the best example of this flag.

The Third Flag Act of 1818 brought the number of stripes back to the original thirteen and declared that a new star would be added for each new state. There were no instructions for how the stars should be placed, however, so some flagmakers put them in a circle, some placed them in lines, and some made the individual stars into one big star.

This pattern for a thirteen-star flag was named after John Trumbull, a Revolutionary War patriot, artist, and personal aide to George Washington. The flag is made of wool bunting with cotton stars and has been lovingly cared for and carefully patched over the years, including the bottom corner of the fly end, which was repaired with patterned dress fabric.

(Text and photo, permission of The Rare Flags Collection)

The pattern on this flag was designed by Francis Hopkinson of New Jersey, a signer of the Declaration of Independence. Even though it represents the original thirteen colonies, the flag pictured here dates to the Civil War period. In owner Anthony Iasso's words, "Its obvious wear, unpretentious utilitarian style and rich coloration elevates the flag to a picture perfect rendition of what one would imagine when they imagine Old Glory." *(Text and photo, permission of The Rare Flags Collection)*

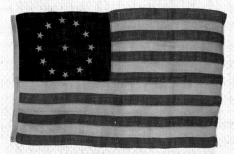

This Maryland or "Cowpens" flag, named after the Battle of Cowpens in the Revolutionary War, is an excellent example of the historic flags that Americans have continually produced and flown to celebrate our nation's history. It has the words "St. Louis World's Fair" stamped lightly on the hoist, so it was most likely produced to be sold as a souvenir at the 1904 St. Louis World's Fair, the largest international fair held to date; St. Louis was also the venue for the 1904 Summer Olympic Games. *(Text and photo, permission of The Rare Flags Collection)*

In 1912, President William Howard Taft decided that the stars should be in rows and that a single point of each star should point upward. At last, a uniform flag! Well, almost . . . two more executive orders followed. On January 3, 1959, with the addition

This flag, with just fifteen stars and eleven stripes, is one of the rarest and earliest American flags known. It dates to the period of the Second Flag Act of 1794, which decreed that the flag have fifteen stars and fifteen stripes. One of the most famous of this flag's counterparts, also with a count of fifteen stars, is the Star-Spangled Banner, sewn by Mary Pickersgill in Baltimore in 1813. It survives along with this flag as one of just four or five known period fifteen-star flags remaining today. *(Text and photo, permission of The Rare Flags Collection)*

This flag is one of the earliest examples of the beloved "Great Star" pattern of American flags, and it is also one of the earliest printed flags known. Captain Samuel Reid, an American naval hero of the War of 1812, designed the Great Star pattern in 1818 as a novel way of incorporating the growing number of stars into the canton. Reid's experience as a mariner, having to determine the nationality of a ship at long distances from its flag, was most likely why he designed such a bold, beautiful, and easily recognizable pattern. *(Text and photo, permission of The Rare Flags Collection)*

of Alaska, our forty-ninth state, President Dwight Eisenhower ordered the stars to be set in seven rows of seven stars apiece, staggered across and down the field.

And again, on August 21, 1959, Eisenhower ordered a new flag after Hawaii was admitted to the union on August 18. Five horizontal rows of six stars each alternate with four staggered rows of five stars apiece. This flag took us into the twenty-first century and is the one we fly today.

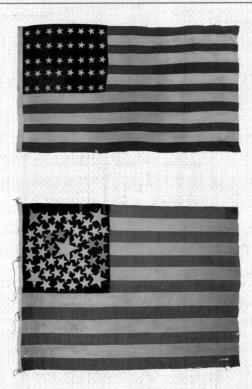

During the late 1880s the United States grew from thirty-eight states to forty-four states in less than a year, adding the following six states in order: North Dakota, South Dakota, Montana, Washington, Idaho, and Wyoming. Because flagmakers did not expect the Dakotas to enter as two states, they made a large quantity of thirty-nine-star flags but few forty-star flags, as Montana was added to the Union just six days after the Dakotas. This beautiful flag, with its rows of tumbling stars is one of just a handful—perhaps five or fewer—of homemade forty-star flags known. *(Text and photo, permission of The Rare Flags Collection)*

Until the introduction of the forty-eight-star flag with the admission of New Mexico and Arizona in 1912, there was no official pattern for stars on the flag. Americans freely populated the starry constellations of their homemade flags according to their own whims. When the forty-eight-star flag was introduced in 1912, President William Howard Taft issued an executive order establishing the official proportions of the flag and the arrangement of the stars: six horizontal rows of eight, with each star pointing upward. True to the spirit of American individuality, the maker of this flag either ignored the mandated status quo or produced the flag before the executive order. *(Text and photo, permission of The Rare Flags Collection)*

"This flag, which we honor and under which we serve, is the emblem of our unity, our power, our thought and purpose as a nation. It has no other character than that which we give it from generation to generation. The choices are ours. It floats in majestic silence above the hosts that execute those choices, whether in peace or in war. And yet, though silent, it speaks to us—speaks to us of the past, of the men and women who went before us, and of the records they wrote upon it." —**President Woodrow Wilson, June 14, 1917**

Memorial Day

Before Memorial Day, there was Decoration Day, first held on May 30, 1868, as a day to honor those who died in the Civil War with flowers at their graves. The date was selected because flowers would be blossoming all across the country by then.

After the Civil War, many cities in both the North and the South paid tribute to their war dead by decorating soldiers' graves with flowers. After World War I, this commemoration was expanded to include all Americans who had fallen in an American war. In 1971 Congress declared Memorial Day a national holiday and set its date as the last Monday in May.

Coast Guard Cadet Jonas Miller unfurls an American flag alongside veterans of the armed services during a Memorial Day celebration on the deck of the USS *Intrepid* in New York. *(US Coast Guard photo by Seth Johnson)*

For the first time ever, on Memorial Day in 2011, flags adorned the fifty thousand grave markers at Massachusetts National Cemetery in Bourne on Cape Cod. The family of Army Sgt. First Class Jared Monti, who was killed in Afghanistan in 2006, organized the undertaking, assisted by hundreds of volunteers. The cemetery had not permitted flags to be placed near markers but agreed in 2011 to allow them on Memorial Day and Veterans Day.

(Photo credit: Elizabeth Young)

Fleet Week

In the United States, Fleet Week is a celebration to honor and thank the men and women of the Navy, Marine Corps, and Coast Guard. The first Fleet Week was held in San Diego in 1935. The public can take guided tours of the ships that dock for a week in various port cities in the United States, such as San Francisco, New York City, and Charleston, South Carolina. Seattle, Washington, hosts the tradition for a week with its own Seafair, and Oregonians host the Portland Rose Festival. Tourists can visit

Intelligence Spc. Second Class Tashawbaba McHerrin hands an American flag to a child on the ship's flight deck during a Fleet Week open house aboard the USS *Enterprise* (CVN-65) in Port Everglades, Florida. *(Photo credit: US Navy Matthew Keane)*

specially designated ships, thrill over Coast Guard search-and-rescue demonstrations, tap their feet to Marine band concerts, and marvel over the agility and prowess of US Navy helicopter pilots. Fleet Week also gives sailors, servicemen, and servicewomen a chance to take in the sights of the welcoming host city. The festivities are often accompanied by performances by the Blue Angels.

Flag Day

When Bernard Cigrand's students arrived at the Stony Hill School in Ozaukee County, Wisconsin, on June 14, 1885, they had no idea they would be playing a part in creating a national holiday. Cigrand, only nineteen himself, called the day

On Sunday, December 7, 1941, the Japanese navy attacked Pearl Harbor, Hawaii, a territory of the United States, thereby ensuring America's direct participation in World War II on the side of the Allied forces. President Franklin D. Roosevelt called it "a date that will live in infamy." Every December 7, flags around the country are flown at half-staff to remember the day. Other days to fly the flag at half-staff are May 15 for Peace Officers Memorial Day, Memorial Day in May, and September 11 for Patriot Day.

the flag's birthday; it was 108 years after the Continental Congress adopted the flag of the United States in 1777. He had placed a small American flag on his desk and asked his students to write essays about the flag and its meaning to them. From that assignment came Cigrand's three-decade-long campaign to establish a national Flag Day. His hard work paid off in 1916, when President Woodrow Wilson proclaimed Flag Day a national observance. More than thirty years later, in 1949, President Harry S. Truman signed a bill designating June 14 as Flag Day.

The poster for the 140th Flag Day, June 14, 1917. Notice our national emblem, the bald eagle, flying above the flag.
(Library of Congress Prints and Photographs part of the Willard and Dorothy Straight Collection)

The Fourth of July

Also known as Independence Day, July 4, 1776, was the day Benjamin Franklin, Thomas Jefferson, John Hancock, John Adams, and fifty-two other statesmen in the Continental Congress signed the Declaration of Independence and set our country and its two and a half million people on the road to being a sovereign nation, independent from Great Britain. (George Washington did not sign because, as commander in chief of the Continental Army, he was off fighting the revolution.) This, of course, despite the considerable number of colonists who sided with the king, was a cause for great celebration.

Citizens of St. Helena Island, South Carolina, gather to celebrate the Fourth of July in 1939.

(Photo credit: Marion Post Wolcott, 1939, Library of Congress Farm Security Administration/Office of War Information)

On July 5, 1777, John Adams wrote to his daughter:

> *My dear Daughter . . . Yesterday, being the anniversary of American Independence, was celebrated here [in Philadelphia] with a festivity and ceremony becoming the occasion. . . . In the evening, I was walking about the streets for a little fresh air*

and exercise, and was surprised to find the whole city lighting up their candles at the windows. I walked most of the evening, and I think it was the most splendid illumination I ever saw; a few surly houses were dark; but the lights were very universal. Considering the lateness of the design and the suddenness of the execution, I was amazed at the universal joy and alacrity that was discovered, and at the brilliancy and splendour of every part of this joyful exhibition. I had forgot the ringing of bells all day and evening, and the bonfires in the streets, and the fireworks played off.

Almost 250 years later, we still celebrate the day with fireworks, parades, backyard barbecues, concerts, and even a political speech or two.

Armed Forces Day

On August 31, 1949, President Harry S. Truman declared Armed Forces Day. The theme for the new holiday was "Teamed for Defense." The goal was to create a day for Americans to recognize and honor all our military forces: the Army, Navy, Air Force, Coast Guard, and Marine Corps. In his presidential proclamation of February 27, 1950, President Truman stated, "Armed Forces

Armed Forces Day poster with a large flag in the background. Designed by Air Force M.Sgt. Doug Sanderson, this poster was reproduced around the world to help the military celebrate the fiftieth anniversary of its special day.
(Photo credit: US Air Force)

Day, Saturday, May 20, 1950, marks the first combined demonstration by America's defense team of its progress, under the National Security Act, towards the goal of readiness for any eventuality. It is the first parade of preparedness by the unified forces of our land, sea, and air defense." Celebrated on the third Saturday in May with parades, receptions, air shows, speeches, and other festivities, Armed Forces Day is supported by all branches of the military, including the National Guard and Reserve units.

Veterans Day

Tammy Duckworth, former assistant secretary of the Department of Veterans Affairs, talks with a World War II veteran at a ceremony honoring veterans at the World War II Memorial in Washington, D.C., on March 10, 2010. *(Photo by Alexandra Hemmerly-Brown)*

On November 11, 1918, the Allied nations and Germany laid down their arms, ending the hostilities in World War I. Seven months later, on June 18, 1919, the war was officially over when the combatants signed the Treaty of Versailles. In the United States, the first anniversary of the cease-fire was commemorated as Armistice Day, with President Woodrow Wilson declaring, "To us in America, the reflections of Armistice Day will be filled with solemn pride in the heroism of those who died in the country's service and with gratitude for the victory, both because of the thing from which it has freed us and because of the opportunity it has given America to show her sympathy with peace and justice in the councils of the nations."

Nineteen years later Congress officially made Armistice Day—the 11th of November—a national holiday, to further world peace. After the valiant fighting of our troops in World War II and the Korean War, veterans' organizations in 1954 lobbied to change the name of the holiday to "Veterans Day," to remember those Americans who fought in all of our nation's wars.

The Blue Angels

Chances are you or someone you know is one of the more than 427 million spectators who have cheered at a Blue Angels show. The Blue Angels are the United States Navy's flying aerobatic team, thrilling the public with their loops, rolls, tight turns, and inversions, many flown close to the speed of sound. The team is made up of sixteen officers and an enlisted crew of forty-five men and women from the Navy and Marine Corps. Together the team puts on seventy shows a year around the country. A tradition since 1946, the "Blues" today fly the F/A-18 Hornet, coated with special paint that reduces drag and improves air performance. In the diamond formation, the planes fly a mere eighteen inches apart—close enough to reach out and touch.

The US Navy Blue Angels in diamond formation at the Seattle Seafair. *(Photo credit: Todd Vorenkamp, www.tvphoto.com)*

I was on the runway in Blue Angel #6 preparing for takeoff during our first air show since the September 11 attacks had shut down all of aviation. After takeoff on a high performance climb, I completed a split-S maneuver and was afforded my first opportunity to view the crowd from the air. It was a sight I will never forget. Not only was the entire air show crowd a sea of red, white, and blue, but Interstate 35W as far as the eye could see was stopped and cars were pulled over. Everyone was waving the American flag, our symbol of freedom, patriotism, heroism, courage, and sacrifice, the symbol that unites us as a free people. **—CDR Scott A. Kartvedt, US Navy**

The Thunderbirds

What kind of training does it take to fly the Air Force "Fighting Falcon" Thunderbird jet upside down, 200 feet above the ground at 1,500 miles per hour? The team, made up of a dozen officers and more than 120 enlisted Air Force members, serves and trains intensely together for hours a day in preparation for a single air show—a tradition since

The Air Force Thunderbirds perform a pass across air show central during the 2008 "Wings over Charleston" Air Expo at the Charleston Air Force Base, South Carolina. *(Photo credit: US Air Force photo by Senior Airman Nicholas Pilch)*

1953. During shows, the flyers demonstrate precise maneuvers in top-of-the-line aircraft. Thunderbirds travel all over the world to showcase the skills and talent of US airmen.

The War of 1812

In the early 1800s tensions were running high between America and Great Britain. The British restricted trade by the United States, seized American ships, and forced American sailors into the British navy. Finally, President James Madison had enough and in 1812 sought a declaration of war from Congress. After three years of fighting, the conflict was resolved with the Treaty of Ghent, forever cementing US independence. The war also gave us patriotic, colorful stories and anthems. One tells of the courageous first lady Dolley Madison, who stood fast in the White House as British troops reached the nation's capital to set it ablaze. She would not flee until she knew George Washington's portrait was safe. In another, more familiar story, Francis Scott Key was stranded on a British ship in the Chesapeake Bay. The sight of our flag waving over Fort McHenry after a British attack inspired Key to compose the lyrics for "The Star-Spangled Banner."

Revenue Cutters

The United States Coast Guard is almost as old as the nation itself. In 1790 the nation's first Congress authorized the construction of a "system of cutters" or Revenue Cutters to protect the nation's revenue by deterring smuggling and enforcing federal tariff and trade laws. Alexander Hamilton, who at the early age of thirty-two was the first secretary of the treasury, insisted upon "thrift and responsibility" to the public. Sailors of the Revenue Cutter Service were thus "servants of the people" and fought the French and English, battled pirates, and much more. During the War of 1812, these cutters protected our coasts and ports, assisted the Navy, and participated in "brown water" combat operations (those in rivers or close to shore), a mission that continues today. During one such mission in 1814, the Revenue Cutter *Eagle* ran

A watercolor painting by Irwin Bevan that depicts the capture of the Revenue Cutter *Surveyor*. *(Credit: The Mariners' Museum, Newport News, VA, Capture of the Surveyor, June 12, 1813. Artist: Irwin Bevan)*

ashore on Negros Head, Long Island, while battling the HMS *Dispatch*. The *Eagle*'s crew "dragged some of the cutter's guns onto a high bluff" and fought courageously, according to the Coast Guard website. The *Eagle*'s American flag was shot away three times and replaced each time by volunteers from the crew.

The American Civil War, 1861–1865

War is never more tragic than when it pits brother against brother, sister against sister. When campaigning for the Senate, Abraham Lincoln declared, "Government cannot endure, permanently half slave, half free." By November 1860, he was elected president, but even before his inauguration the following March, seven Southern states had seceded from the Union and formed the Confederacy; later in 1861, four more states would secede. The war against neighbors and states had begun. The Southern states believed that states' rights should be more sovereign than federal rights. They wanted the right to determine taxation, tariffs, and, of course, the issue of slavery, for themselves.

A lithograph from 1905 depicts President Abraham Lincoln giving his Gettysburg Address at the dedication of the Gettysburg National Cemetery, November 19, 1863. *(Photo credit: Library of Congress)*

Lincoln was resolved to preserve the Union. Through the long and bitter war, and the raising of the Confederate flag over the states that had seceded, he was relentless in pursuit of this goal. The North kept the Union flag, with all of its stars, flying during our nation's darkest time.

With the Emancipation Proclamation in 1863, Lincoln declared slaves within the Confederacy forever free. After the "War Between the States" ended in 1865, slavery was abolished everywhere in the nation. Rebuilding our country took years, especially in the South, where much of the fighting occurred.

On November 19, 1863, in Gettysburg, Pennsylvania, Lincoln delivered his Gettysburg Address. "The world will little note, nor long remember what we say here," he said. But the world did note and did remember, and the flag once again flew over the states as a united country.

Soldiers are known to have carried with them small parade flags, sometimes sewn into their uniforms, upon which they wrote messages. The soldier who carried the flag shown is unknown, but he was most likely assigned to Company A, Twelfth New York Cavalry and was captured with Private William H. Courtney. They were imprisoned at the Andersonville Prison in Andersonville, Georgia, where Courtney died on July 14, 1864. The soldier carried this flag and wrote on it, according to the Rare Flags website, "Private Courtney's date of death and the grave number to preserve his memory and to one day present to his loved ones." The survival of these flags is extremely rare, serving as reminders of the horrid conditions the soldiers endured in the prison camp and making this small, beautiful flag one of the most personal and poignant relics to have survived the American Civil War.

This is a thirteen-star flag found at the Andersonville Prison after the Civil War. *(Memorial of Private William Courtney, 1864. Text and photo, permission of The Rare Flag Collection)*

World War I, 1914–1918

World War I had been raging in Europe for years when President Woodrow Wilson realized that the United States could not maintain its neutrality in "the Great War." In April 1917, he presented his case to Congress for a declaration of war against Germany so that the world would "be made safe for democracy." After the United States entered the war, Wilson provided a "blueprint" for "peace negotiations in his War Aims and Peace Terms speech—also known as the Fourteen Points. By November 1918 Germany signed the armistice.

An African-American soldier proudly stands in front of the American flag during World War I. *(Library of Congress Gladstone Collection of African American Photographs)*

This poster from approximately 1917 encourages young men to join the armed forces. *(Willard and Dorothy Straight Collection, Library of Congress Prints and Photographs)*

If it's worth living under It's worth fighting for **ENLIST TODAY**

The last goal Wilson sought was the establishment of "a general association of nations . . . affording mutual guarantees of political independence and territorial integrity to great and small states alike." An association of countries—this was a new idea. Could the nations of the world join together, for the greater good of the world,

While forty-eight-star flags are common, this flag, marked with the date of Armistice Day (November 11), is extremely rare and may be the only one of its kind. The formal end of hostilities in World War I came in the eleventh hour of the eleventh day of the eleventh month of 1918. The day, originally known as Armistice Day, was marked by President Woodrow Wilson as a day to honor the heroism of those who died in the war. Armistice Day became a recurring holiday in 1938, and in 1954 under President Dwight Eisenhower, the holiday was legally changed to Veterans Day, a day to celebrate the sacrifices and heroism of all veterans from all wars. *(Text and photo, permission of The Rare Flag Collection)*

to resolve problems, to monitor issues, and to help ensure a safer life for all? Wilson believed it was possible. After the war, he included in the Versailles Treaty a provision for the covenant of the League of Nations, asking, "Dare we reject it and break the heart of the world?"

World War II, 1939–1945

The American flag was a powerful symbol during World War II. For Americans on the home front and for those fighting in foreign lands, it was a beacon of hope and strength. Howard Schnauber said in an interview at the Fort Collins Museum, "As a young Marine in combat . . . we saw a lot of things that a human body shouldn't see." But seeing the flag waving on foreign lands, on the decks of American ships, leading the troops and showing the way for those so far from home, was a sight they never forgot.

The "Big Three," from left to right, Prime Minister Winston Churchill, President Franklin D. Roosevelt, and Premier Joseph Stalin, meet for the Crimean Conference at the Livadia Palace near Yalta in Crimea, Ukraine, in February 1945. *(US Signal Corps, Library of Congress Prints and Photographs)*

President Franklin Delano Roosevelt and Prime Minister Winston Churchill of the United Kingdom led the way for millions of soldiers and civilians with their now famous wartime words:

> WE SHALL NOT FLAG OR FAIL. WE SHALL GO ON TO THE END. WE SHALL FIGHT IN FRANCE, WE SHALL FIGHT ON THE SEAS AND OCEANS, WE SHALL FIGHT WITH GROWING CONFIDENCE AND GROWING STRENGTH IN THE AIR, WE SHALL DEFEND OUR ISLAND, WHATEVER THE COST MAY BE. WE SHALL FIGHT ON THE BEACHES, WE SHALL FIGHT ON THE LANDING GROUNDS, WE SHALL FIGHT IN THE FIELDS AND IN THE STREETS, WE SHALL FIGHT IN THE HILLS; WE SHALL NEVER SURRENDER.
>
> —*WINSTON CHURCHILL, JUNE 4, 1940, "WE SHALL FIGHT ON THE BEACHES" SPEECH TO THE HOUSE OF COMMONS FOLLOWING OPERATION DYNAMO AND THE EVACUATION OF 338,000 ALLIED TROOPS TO ENGLISH SHORES*

> "WE LOOK FORWARD TO A WORLD FOUNDED UPON FOUR ESSENTIAL HUMAN FREEDOMS . . . FREEDOM OF SPEECH AND EXPRESSION . . . FREEDOM OF EVERY PERSON TO WORSHIP GOD IN HIS OWN WAY . . . FREEDOM FROM WANT . . . FREEDOM FROM FEAR."
>
> —*FRANKLIN DELANO ROOSEVELT, JANUARY 6, 1941, STATE OF THE UNION ADDRESS, "FOUR FREEDOMS SPEECH"*

In July 1942, the United We Stand campaign, which featured the flag and the flag's role at home and abroad, reinforced what it meant to be American during a time of war. It inspired all Americans to support our nation's ideals through service and sacrifice. It has continued to be a rallying call for Americans during times of war or emergency. This streamer was prepared by the Office of Emergency Management (OEM) for use in defense plants throughout the nation. *(Library of Congress Prints & Photographs Division)*

> *"When I think of our flag, I think of those who have gone before us who have given their lives to keep our flag waving for freedom. My Uncle Ernie, who died in France in September of 1944 and received the Bronze Star for valor."* —**Jack Shea, California**

Korean War, 1950–1953

It was June 1950. World War II had ended five years earlier and a "young Cold War suddenly turned hot, bloody and expensive," according to the Naval History and Heritage Command website. On June 25, North Korea invaded South Korea, bringing about a United Nations "police action against the aggressors," who were part of a global Communist challenge.

Beginning in July 1950, the United States readied World War II–era aircraft, ships, and equipment for service. Troops deployed. "The veterans of the Korean War," which had stabilized by July 1953, "saved the Republic of Korea from a tragic fate," wrote Theodore F. Low, chairman of the Korean War Memorial Commission of Rhode Island, in an article published in 1998 in the *Providence Journal*.

"The American Flag has been a tapestry of stars and stripes in every courthouse, emblematic of the Constitution and the Bill of Rights, signifying that an individual's life, liberty, and property are always secure." The building in the picture, behind the flag, is the Providence County Courthouse. Judge Robert D. Krause, who has served more than twenty-five years on that court, is the senior associate justice. *(Judge Robert D. Krause)*

The Korean War Monument of Rhode Island, shown in the photo on page 83 by Judge Robert D. Krause of the Rhode Island Superior Court, includes a Memorial Walkway made from bricks and engraved with the names of American men and women who served in Korea. The monument was established "to express the everlasting gratitude of the people of Rhode Island to all those who took part in the Korean War—to those who survived and to those who gave their lives" Low wrote. "Some have called [it] 'America's Forgotten War'; its veterans in many ways were also forgotten."

The monument was part of the healing process, Low explained. Both the monument and the walkway inspire veterans and their families to overcome the "spiritual and psychological wounds" they suffered during the war. Future generations are able to learn about these earlier generations of Americans who left a legacy reminding us of the human cost of defending freedom—as depicted by the bronze sculpture of a soldier in the center of the memorial. The lone soldier is on guard, isolated, yet "conveys . . . loyalty to his country," Low wrote. "It is dark and bitter cold. . . . While his head is down . . . his eyes are staring into the distance. . . . He exemplifies the fact that freedom is not free."

Vietnam War, 1964–1973

American troops fought alongside the South Vietnamese in the villages and jungles of Vietnam in an attempt to prevent the spread of communism by the North Vietnamese forces. This war was the continuation of a struggle that had been going on for several decades involving other countries. The United States, with pressure from the American public—including thousands of students on college campuses—withdrew most of its troops by 1972, but it wasn't until the Paris Peace Accords of 1973 that a cease-fire was negotiated. Today the Socialist Republic of Vietnam is a single-party state led by the Communist Party.

"Not seeing the flag where you most expect it to be is a terrible moment. During my service as a patrol boat commanding officer in Vietnam, I remember being recalled to port during a heavy monsoon. We were as far from our base as assignments took us, and on the way back to base, in nightmarish sea conditions, we literally had our national ensign blown away by the storm. As we limped back into port and finally out of harm's way, the first thing we saw was Old Glory flying strong and true from the masthead of our mother ship. Pride welled up in our entire crew, and the first thing accomplished upon docking was returning a new national ensign to its proper place. It's fascinating how much memories never fade." —**Adm. James Loy, US Coast Guard Commandant (Ret.)**

A small flag reflects against the names inscribed on the Vietnam Veterans Memorial. Thousands gathered in Washington, D.C., on November 11, 2002, to mark the twentieth anniversary of the Vietnam Veterans Memorial Wall's dedication. *(US Navy Photographer's Mate First Class Brien Aho)*

The War on Terror, 2001–Present

A December 2006 Christmas card picture from Baghdad, Iraq. The 447th EOD Flight (an explosive ordnance disposal flight) provided IED- and route-clearance for missions in and around Baghdad.

(Photo credit: Brad Kline)

Shortly after the terrorist strikes on American soil on September 11, 2001, the scope of the threat and the military operations required to confront it necessitated waging a new kind of war: "a war on terrorism." Nine days after the attacks, President George W. Bush addressed Congress, saying, "Our war on terror . . . will not end until every terrorist group of global reach has been found, stopped, and defeated."

> *"Our country was founded on some pretty lofty ideas that at the time were pretty revolutionary and counter to conventional wisdom: that the average person could have a say in government, could work to make a life for themselves unmolested by government. Our country has done its share of silly and embarrassing things in its two hundred–plus years, but I still think that we are a beacon for many around the world. Our flag is the clearest symbol of that beacon."* **—Dave Teska, Kansas**

The United States and Great Britain led an international military coalition—made up of members of the North Atlantic Treaty Organization (NATO) and non-NATO countries—to combat terrorist organizations. The coalition would fight the war on terror by defeating terrorists such as Osama bin Laden and Abu Musab al-Zarqawi and destroying their organizations and training camps. Coalition forces moved into Afghanistan in October 2001, thereby initiating Operation Enduring Freedom (OEF).

A young boy awaits the return of his father, a pilot with the Fourth Fighter Squadron, on April 15, 2011, at Hill Air Force Base, Utah. The arriving airmen are the first of a team returning from a six-month deployment to Bagram Air Base, Afghanistan. *(US Air Force photo by S.Sgt. Renae Saylock)*

After the Gulf War in Iraq (August 1990 to February 1991), coalition forces returned in 2003 for the beginning of Operation Iraqi Freedom (OIF). The air campaign was followed by a US-led ground invasion. Baghdad, Iraq's capital city, fell along with Saddam Hussein and his government. But an insurgency rose up in opposition and sectarian killings wracked the country before a troop surge gradually restored order. On December 15, 2011, the United States officially declared the war in Iraq over, and three days later the last US combat troops left the country. Plans call for the withdrawal of US troops in Afghanistan by 2014.

Joplin, Missouri, May 22, 2011

Joplin was devastated on May 22, 2011, by an EF-5 tornado with winds greater than two hundred miles per hour. The tornado killed more than 150 people and injured more than one thousand, making it "the deadliest since modern recordkeeping began in 1950," according to the National Weather Service.

Americans responded.

A battered flag is a powerful symbol of hope and resilience after the Joplin tornado.

(Photo credit: whitneyscottphotography.com)

Organizations such as the Red Cross, the Salvation Army, the Federal Emergency Management Agency, and the Convoy of Hope disaster response team had shelters up and running within hours. Emergency vehicles were ready with food, water, and relief supplies. Health workers arrived to tend to the wounded, talk to the bereaved, and monitor the air for the presence of asbestos.

The Missouri Army and Air National Guard helped rescue dozens of people who were trapped in homes or under debris. Army Spc. Jeffrey Price, a heavy equipment operator for the 294th Engineer Company, Missouri Army National Guard from Carthage, searched for

(Photo credit: whitneyscottphotography.com)

> *"The flag to me has always been this 'idea' of America. I'm reminded of the Norman Rockwell ideal of soldiers peeling potatoes and children riding bicycles with streamers and fireworks with a cold glass of lemonade. It's not that the flag doesn't represent that side of America—because it does, but it took a tragedy in my town to bring me to a new depth of appreciation for it.*
>
> *On May 22, 2011, Joplin, Missouri, was hit with the worst tornado this country has seen in more than fifty years . . . an F5 nearly a mile wide that stayed on the ground for over six miles. More than 150 people were killed. Seven thousand homes and two thousand businesses destroyed. Our city was deeply wounded.*
>
> *I think now I will forever see the flag at half-mast. I will remember it hanging from broken windows and shredded tree trunks and the tailgates of trucks full of relief supplies. I will see the dirt-crusted hands and warm smiling faces of volunteers from all over the United States who rushed in with semitrucks full of tarps and blankets and toothpaste (you wouldn't believe all the toothpaste!). I will remember the love and care given to our community in a time when it was so desperately needed. It's the people I will remember. It's the people who are America—the people this flag represents."* **—Whitney Scott, photographer**

victims after the roof of the Wal-Mart store where he was working was blown off. He and his supervisor, a former Marine, rescued sixty people from the store. "Some people would call him a hero, but to hear Spc. Jeffrey Price tell it, he was just doing his job," stated an article by Army Sgt. Jon D. Dougherty.

Other National Guard infantrymen knocked on doors to make sure residents had the best information and resources.

Haiti, January 12, 2010

On January 12, 2010, a 7.0 magnitude earthquake struck Haiti, the western part of the island of Hispaniola in the Caribbean. According to the US Geological Survey, officials estimate that the quake killed approximately 316,000 people, injured 300,000 more, and displaced upward of 1.3 million. The US military and American

Haitian Americans sit on board a C-17 Globemaster III on January 18, 2010, flying from Toussaint Louverture International Airport in Port-au-Prince, Haiti, to Orlando Sanford International Airport in Florida. The C-17 crew is assigned to the 729th Airlift Squadron at March Air Reserve Base, California. The aircraft is from the 452nd Air Mobility Wing at March ARB. *(US Air Force photo by S.Sgt. Jacob N. Bailey)*

response agencies participated in a record humanitarian effort to rescue, assist, and recover those trapped or unable to help themselves. Within hours America deployed service members and resources. Surveillance teams, rescue helicopters, a team of military engineers, operational planners, communication specialists, and a command and control group arrived on the scene, setting up an airlift and providing aid. Besides bringing medical care and supplies, the US military sought to make sure that airports and seaports were open and ready to receive the flood of aid that would pour into Haiti in the days after the quake. In addition to dropping supplies, the Air Force was the first to arrive on land, with a team of specially trained airmen who worked to get the destroyed airport running again.

The Army's Eighty-second Airborne Division, a Marine expeditionary unit, the hospital ship USNS *Comfort*, and the aircraft carrier USS *Carl Vinson* all launched swiftly to help. The medical facilities on the ships were equipped to treat hundreds of casualties, with six emergency operating rooms.

The US Coast Guard also quickly made preparations to deploy on ships and by air. The Coast Guard cutter *Forward* reached Haiti the morning after the quake, and the crew worked to evaluate the damage at the port in Port-au-Prince, providing critical command and control capabilities for the massive multiagency response. Coast Guard aircrews from Florida, Hawaii, California, Michigan, and Alabama conducted overflights, while other cutters like the *Tahoma* and *Mohawk* treated hundreds until the

Comfort arrived. During the weeks that followed, the service members worked round the clock to provide relief supplies and medical aid, even quickly establishing a makeshift trauma unit that triaged hundreds of injured people in conjunction with the Haitian Coast Guard in Killick.

Although the military's first mission is one of combat operations, in situations such as the Haitian earthquake, the men and women in the armed forces are trained equally well to be the first line of defense in saving lives and aiding survivors.

Hurricane Katrina, August 29, 2005

US Coast Guard Petty Officer Second Class Shawn Beaty of Long Island, New York, looks for survivors in the wake of Hurricane Katrina as he flies in an HH-60J Jayhawk helicopter. *(Photo credit: Petty Officer Cangemi, USCG)*

In late August 2005, a tropical storm developed over the Bahamas and moved toward Florida. It was named Katrina. The storm powered up to a Category 5 hurricane packing winds of 175 miles per hour. When it hit the city of New Orleans, Louisiana, on August 29, it had become a Category 3 storm, but it still dealt a devastating punch across the Gulf Coast. The storm surge and winds, caused flood walls to break, ravaging the region.

Responding to the destruction across Louisiana, Mississippi, and Alabama were more than sixty thousand military forces, including active duty, reserves, and the National Guard, who evacuated more than sixty thousand people, rescued more than fourteen thousand, and treated thousands stranded by the storm. Twenty Navy vessels and seven Coast Guard ships rushed to the area, including the USS *Whidbey Island*, which delivered six floating bridges to replace those destroyed in New Orleans, and the USS *Tortuga*, whose crew helped conduct evacuations, distribute food and water, and transport support troops. "Every state in the union and every territory contributed to the National Guard's response," the National Guard Bureau said.

The first orders were to save and then sustain lives. As the world watched, their courageous work not only saved thousands of lives, but also shone a light on some of the "finest hours" of innovation and service by the military and other agencies in what was one of the largest disaster responses ever.

The Bering Sea Patrol

Going to work on the waters off Alaska can be a dangerous yet exciting endeavor. Dating back to the mid-1800s, Bering Sea Patrols have provided adventurous work, despite the poor food and living conditions. Cuttermen from the US Revenue Cutter Service and US Lighthouse Service, later known as the US Coast Guard, annually journeyed north in May from west coast ports to the Aleutian and Pribilof Islands or popular fishing areas in the Bering Sea. There they endured fierce gales, arctic cold, fog, and ice to perform rescues, provide medical aid, and monitor the fishing and hunting of marine mammals to prevent their extinction. Islands had to be visited by small cutter boats, making landings hazardous. During some of these attempts to go ashore, according to an article by Dennis L. Noble on the US Coast Guard website, "cuttermen were lost . . . and buried in remote, unmarked graves." Living aboard a Revenue Cutter was equally life-threatening. In 1896, the ship's log officer on the vessel *Perry* wrote:

> Seaman C. C. Mauethrop went aloft to clear the pennant. He reached the truck
> and endeavored for the space of a minute, to break out the pennant, when, for
> some unaccountable reason, he fell to the deck and was instantly killed. Seaman
> Mauethrop, incidentally, on April 18, 1896, unhesitatingly dived into a high sea
> to pass a line and assist a shipmate who was so numbed that he could not help
> himself aboard when his small boat capsized.

Others who died while serving on the patrol "were buried where they met their fate, or they were buried at sea and thus nothing remains to mark their final resting spot," Noble wrote. The cemetery for one city in Alaska, however, called Unalaska, contains the burial sites of some United States Revenue Cutter Service and United States Coast Guard enlisted men, including Mauethrop. His grave exists, Noble wrote, because "the sailor's shipmates throughout the patrol took up a collection to erect a stone marker in his memory." The *esprit de corps* among sailors appealed to the cuttermen, who decided to serve this remote duty despite its costs and lack of amenities.

In the past on July Fourth, cutters in Unalaska would "send an honor guard to fire a salute over these graves," according to Noble's article. That tradition stopped with World War II, and soon after cuttermen there were forgotten until the group Unalaska Native Pride began a restoration project in 1989 to preserve the grounds and mark the graves of the sailors. Patrols in the Bering Sea continue today with near-constant Coast Guard presence enforcing maritime laws, providing search and rescue and humanitarian aid, and supporting scientific research—much like the pioneering sailors of the Revenue Cutter Service who began patrolling these remote waters in 1865.

In 2011, Capt. Matt Gimple, commanding officer of the USCGC *Hamilton*, based in San Diego, California, patrolled the Bering Sea and made port calls to Dutch Harbor, Unalaska. There, he and several of his crew replaced the weathered American flag and Coast Guard standard that was half gone but still flying above the old cemetery and Bering Sea Monument. *(Photo credit: US Coast Guard Steven T. Sumner FSCS, USCG Food Service Officer, and input for story provided by Matt Gimple, Captain, US Coast Guard and Commanding Officer USCGC* Hamilton)

"Some of my earliest recollections are of my grandfather raising the national ensign outside his home at 0800 every morning. He was a World War I veteran, member of the local VFW, retired blue-collar worker from the 'rust belt' region of the country. On occasion I became his color guard, marching alongside him from the side door to the flagpole. He taught me how to attach and raise the ensign, salute, and respect our country's flag. When he died, I was still too small to help carry his casket; instead I marched in front of the procession, once again his color guard. Now as a father and assistant scoutmaster for our local Boy Scout troop, I proudly march behind the national ensign with my children each holiday. Old Glory ties me and my family to the long line of patriotic citizens that served our country in war and peace." —**Capt. Matt Gimple, Commanding Officer, USCGC _Hamilton_ (WHEC-715), Ohio**

US Navy Divers

Most of the work done by the Navy's Mobile Diving and Salvage Units One (MDSU-1) and Two (MDSU-2), which were created in 1966 during the Vietnam War, is unseen and unsung. Their mission, according to the MDSU-1 website, is to "rapidly deploy combat ready, expeditionary warfare capable, specialized dive teams" to clear waterways and provide underwater repairs and salvage operations all over the world. When the Japanese fishing vessel _Ehime Maru_ sank in 2001, MDSU-1 was there. Two years later the unit deployed for Operation Iraqi Freedom, conducting "combat harbor clearance in the port of Umm Qasr, Iraq . . . [and] removing derelict Iraqi patrol boats," according to the MDSU-1 website. In recent years MDSU-2 divers have taken part in events of national significance and loss, like the recovery of victims of TWA Flight 800 off Long Island, New York; the terrorist bombing of the USS _Cole_ in Yemen; and the crash of John F. Kennedy Jr.'s plane off Martha's Vineyard. Salvage operations have included a spacecraft off the Florida coast, a helicopter from the depths of the Red and port recovery dives in Port-au-Prince after the Haiti earthquake in 2010.

Navy divers also recovered a treasured piece of history during the USS *Monitor* expedition. In 2001, the five-month effort by Navy divers that recovered part of the *Monitor*'s hull and its groundbreaking steam engine took place after years of planning with the National Oceanic and Atmospheric Administration (NOAA) and the Mariners' Museum. During the Civil War, in March 1862, Union sailors aboard the odd-looking, mostly submerged *Monitor* steamed toward the Confederacy's iron battleship CSS *Virginia* to win the battle with a revolving gun turret that revolutionized naval warfare. The *Monitor* was considered the Navy's first modern warship and was instrumental in the pivotal change from sail and wooden ships to those with hulls of steel. During a terrible winter storm later that year off Cape Hatteras—a place that sailors called "the graveyard of the Atlantic"—the *Monitor* sank.

Navy divers planned three phases of dives to the *Monitor*, which rested 240 feet below on the seabed. On the bottom, divers had less than twenty-five minutes to get to the work site and perform their tasks in swift currents. The depth

Petty Officer Julius McManus, assigned to Mobile Diving and Salvage Unit One, plants an American flag on the site where an American World War II military aircraft crashed into the Pacific Ocean. Deep-sea divers are assigned to Joint POW/MIA Accounting Command (JPAC) in the effort to account for all Americans missing as a result of the nation's past conflicts. *(Photo credit: US Navy Mass Communications Specialist Second Class Christopher Perez)*

of the dive was no problem for the elite set of talented men and women, who were in top physical condition from constant weightlifting, wearing heavy gear, and tugging bundles of "umbilicals" (air supply hoses) connected to their dive suits.

> *"The feeling I get when taps is played or I'm on a military base and all the cars and people stop as morning colors is observed was similar to the feeling I had diving on the USS* Monitor. *We brought down the American flag to the shipwreck to observe and recognize the sailors who died with the ship. It's an ever so brief but important moment to stop to recognize those who believed in our country and died for it. It is that pride embodied in the symbol of our great flag."* —**Capt. Gina Harden, US Navy, Virginia**

On the USS *Monitor* expedition, Navy divers brought the American flag to rest for a moment with the ship and its history, and contemporary Navy sailors felt a camaraderie with their counterparts from the Civil War. As the flag rose again to the surface, it would be prized along with the memories of our rich history and the sight of treasure rescued from the deep.

Washington's Crossing: The Story behind the Art

There is usually a story behind the creation of a work of art. Those that capture our imagination and connect us to a moment in history tend to remain part of our treasured memories. From history lessons or from visiting the work displayed in New York, many people are familiar with and admire the 1850 painting *Washington Crossing the Delaware* by Emanuel Leutze, a German-American immigrant. According to David Hackett Fischer in his book, *Washington's Crossing* (Oxford University Press, 2004), Leutze's story behind the artwork was personal and patriotic. He hoped to see the

This painting, *Washington Crossing the Delaware*, hangs in the Metropolitan Museum of Art in New York. This is a photo by Eastman Johnson. *(Photo credit: Art Resource, NY ART39923)*

revolutions occurring across Europe in 1848 succeed. Leutze, explains Fischer, thought "a painting to encourage Europe" during its struggles would be best represented by "the example of the American Revolution." Much like the American flag flying above Fort McHenry in 1814 inspired the writing of "The Star Spangled Banner," Leutze found his influence in a poem by Ferdinand Freilgart called "Ça Ira," which, according to Fischer's book, "created the image of a vessel filled with determined men":

> You ask astonished: "What's her name?"
> To this question there's but one solution,
> And in Austria and Prussia it's the same:
> The ship is called: "Revolution!"

> "The flag of the United States is a sign. Like any other sort of sign, whether it be directing traffic or advertising a store or something else, our flag points to certain places. Often a school, a post office, a police station, or some other fixture of civil society or government is marked with a flag. Abroad, it is a sign for our ships, our embassies, and our bags of food aid. But our flag is more than just a sign marking some place or object.
>
> "It is a symbol for ideas: the ideas of America, the idea of a nation that believes in individual liberty and in the common good. The idea of a nation that believes it has a larger purpose in history: to be an example of liberty and a refuge for those who seek it. The idea of a nation that believes it can bring to life the opportunities of the future and above all, the flag stands for the idea of a nation that recognizes its imperfections and continues the work of building a more perfect union."
>
> **—Eric Q. Mooring, Eagle Scout**

Invigorated and resolute, Leutze began to paint the work in 1848 and persisted even when the European revolutions failed. Fischer identified Leutze's shift in "mood," noticing that "his colors turned somber, and the painting centered on the theme of struggle more than one of triumph."

Heat and smoke from a fire in Leutze's studio damaged the canvas, which is 149 by 255 inches, leaving the figures of General Washington and James Monroe hazy. Nonetheless, the painting was exhibited and quite well received. In 1942, however, a bombing raid by the British air force destroyed the painting, which was hanging in the Bremen Art Museum in Germany, "in what some have seen as a final act of retribution for the American Revolution," wrote Fischer.

Leutze, though, had painted a second, full-size version of the work, which came to America in 1851, stirring a young nation. The masterpiece made an impression on tens of thousands while exhibited in New York and Washington, D.C., in the Rotunda of the National Capitol. According to Fischer, Americans in the North saw it as "a symbol of freedom and union" while Southerners praised it for its message of "liberty and independence." During the Civil War, the Union side used the painting as a fund-raiser.

"The presence of an African American in the boat was not an accident; the artist was a strong abolitionist," Fischer wrote. Leutze saw that the US war for independence had had a global impact, and he realized that through his artwork, he could show others that "the little battles of the American Revolution were conflicts between large historical processes," as Fischer wrote. Under Washington's leadership, free men had served as active participants in the creation of a new nation. As Washington himself wrote in a letter to Lord Stirling on January 19, 1777, "A people unused to restraint must be led; they will not be drove." This lesson was learned from experience. For it was barely a month before, when many believed that the colonists' cause was close to defeat, that Washington stood up on that boat and led the people and their revolution as he guided his crew across the Delaware.

The flag, which accompanied the vessel that pivotal night, was as much a symbol of this leader, this revolution, and the unification of America's future as General Washington himself.

Students at Bluewater Elementary School in Niceville, Florida, completed a study of the American flag's history and had fun designing their own.

(Photo credit: Robyn Bomar)

The Iwo Jima Memorial

The island of Iwo Jima was the site of one of the fiercest battles of World War II. The key to taking the island, one of the last remaining Japanese outposts, lay with the capture and control of Mount Suribachi, an inactive volcano. After days of shelling by American forces, the US Marines were given the difficult task of taking the mountain. Days of nonstop, lethal fighting ensued. When the Marines took the summit of Mount Suribachi on February 23, 1945, they flew a small American flag. Later that day, a contingent of six men raised a more prominent flag, and Joe Rosenthal captured that feat in a Pulitzer Prize–winning photo that remains one of the most iconic war images. Rosenthal's photo inspired a sculpture designed by Felix W. de Weldon, US Navy—the Marine Corps War Memorial in Arlington, Virginia, which honors all Marines who have died defending America.

"My grandfather, Hugh Willoughby, fought in World War II and in 1915 for the British Royal Navy. He believed in this country so much that he boarded a ship in Great Britain to head to the United States to start his life here. He became one of the designers of the statue of Iwo Jima, a symbol of our commitment, strength, and love of this country." —Alis Willoughby

(Photo credit: Bruce Hugh Willoughby, USMC retired)

The American Flag, Baseball, and the National Anthem

There is a long-honored tradition that before each baseball game, players and spectators stand, face the flag, and sing our national anthem. This started long before the 1931 petition with six million signatures that persuaded Congress and President Herbert Hoover to sign off on the bill making "The Star-Spangled Banner" our anthem. This tradition of baseball, the flag, and the national anthem started at a Boston Red Sox–Chicago Cubs World Series game in 1918, during World War I, as was reported on page 14 of the *New York Times* on September 6, 1918. Read all about it here!

RED SOX BEAT CUBS IN INITIAL GAME OF WORLD'S SERIES

Far different from any incident that has ever occurred in the history of baseball was the great moment of the first world's series game between the Chicago Cubs and the Boston Red Sox, which came at Comiskey Park this afternoon during the seventh-inning stretch. As the crowd of 19,274 spectators—the smallest that has witnessed the diamond classic in many years—stood up to take their afternoon yawn that has been the privilege and custom of baseball fans for many generations, the band broke forth to the strains of "The Star-Spangled Banner."

The yawn was checked and heads were bared as the ballplayers turned quickly about and faced the music. Jackie Fred Thomas of the US Navy was at attention, as he stood erect, with his eyes set on the flag fluttering at the top of the lofty pole in right field. First the song was taken up by a few, then others joined, and when the final notes came, a great volume of melody rolled across the field. It was at the very end that the onlookers exploded into thunderous applause and rent the air with a cheer that marked the highest point of the day's enthusiasm.

The mind of the baseball fan was on the war. The patriotic outburst following the singing of the national anthem was far greater than the upheaval of emotion which greeted Babe Ruth, the Boston southpaw when he conquered Hippo Jim Vaughn and the Cubs in a seething flinging duel by a score of 1 to 0. The cheers for America's stirring song were greater even than the demonstration offered Vaughn when he twice made the mighty Ruth whiff the air.

Baseball and "The Star-Spangled Banner" caught on in full force during World War II when support for our troops fighting overseas rose as one long cheer from the bleachers before each game.

George Rodrigue's GOD BLESS AMERICA

On September 11, 2001, the American people experienced something that few could have imagined. At the moment the planes struck, our bedrock, our beliefs, and our very existence as we knew it was challenged. We had to absorb, to regroup, and to pull out of ourselves a fierceness and a commitment to our Founding Fathers' original vision, and then we had to adjust and carry on. We each found our own way to do this. Artist George Rodrigue used his immense talent to create an image that has found its way around the world and raised millions for the American Red Cross.

Here's what he said about his piece:

> *On the night of September 11, 2001, like Americans everywhere, I sat in shock over the events of the day. As I've done many times in my life, I turned to my easel and paints for comfort.*
>
> *At 5 a.m. the next morning I stared with my wife at the painting I'd just finished. As we looked from each other to the canvas, we knew that I'd made a powerful and accurate statement of our feelings. We discussed our desperation— our wanting to help in some way.*
>
> *I realized as we spoke that in donating the sales from a print of this painting to the relief effort, others might be comforted as they dealt with their own grief and*

God Bless America, 2001, acrylic on canvas, 40 x 40 inches *(Artist: George Rodrigue)*

desire to help. Created in the depths of my personal sadness, the painting reflects the feelings of many, many people.

I first thought to paint the dog black, as if in mourning. Instead I painted it without color at all, the blue joy drained by shock and grief. (Some people have commented that the lack of color reminds them of the television footage of debris-covered people running on the streets of New York City.) For many years the dog has had yellow, happy eyes. On this day, however, the eyes are red, indicating a heavy heart.

I am proud to be from the United States of America. It is our spirit, strong in the symbol of our flag, which will mend our broken hearts and allow us to use these events to strengthen our courage and compassion.

Florida high school student Patrick Saxer paints what the flag means to him. *(Credit: Patrick Saxer)*

The National 9/11 Flag

The National 9/11 Flag is displayed at Giants Stadium on September 13, 2009, before an NFL game between the New York Giants and the Washington Redskins. People across the United States have helped to stitch together the flag as it is being restored. These volunteers have included survivors of the deadly 2009 shooting at Fort Hood, Texas; World War II veterans on the USS *Missouri* in Pearl Harbor, Hawaii; relatives of the Reverend Dr. Martin Luther King Jr.; members of Congress; and thousands of service heroes nationwide. *(Photo credit: New York Says Thank You Foundation)*

"Destroyed in the aftermath of the collapse of the World Trade Center on September 11, 2001, and stitched back together seven years later by tornado survivors in Greensburg, Kansas, the National 9/11 Flag is a living testament to the resilience and compassion of the American people. It is quickly becoming

It's not about what happened on 9/11 so much as it is about what happened on 9/12, says Jeff Parness, CEO of the New York Says Thank You Foundation, speaking about the selfless men and women who put aside their pain to help others deal with theirs. The foundation has brought New York firefighters and volunteers to Illinois, Louisiana, Indiana, Texas, and Kansas in the wake of natural or man-made disasters to repay a nation that came to New York's aid in a time of need. *(Photo credit: New York Says Thank You Foundation)*

recognized as a modern-day version of the Star-Spangled Banner," said Jeff Parness, the director and CEO of the New York Says Thank You Foundation. According to the foundation, more than 300 million Americans have experienced the National 9/11 Flag through local events and national press stories. The flag has not only been

The National 9/11 Flag is one of the largest American flags to fly above the wreckage of Ground Zero. Destroyed in the aftermath of the World Trade Center attacks—and stitched back together over the next decade by tornado survivors, soldiers, and service heroes—"it has become our generation's Star-Spangled Banner," says the New York Says Thank You Foundation. *(Photo credit: New York Says Thank You Foundation)*

witnessed by millions but has also symbolically connected our rich history with relics of the past. The National 9/11 Flag website explains that "a piece of the flag that Abraham Lincoln was laid out on when he was shot at Ford's Theater was stitched into the fabric of the National 9/11 Flag." During the tenth anniversary year of the terrorist attacks, the flag traveled across America. Local heroes in all fifty states helped restore the flag to its thirteen-stripe design. "We also wanted to inspire 300 million Americans with the flag's rich visual history in order to deepen our sense of citizenship and national pride and bolster the spirit of volunteerism on the 9/11 anniversary and year-round," Parness said.

The restored National 9/11 Flag will be added to the collection at the National September 11 Memorial and Museum in New York City.

The Pledge of Allegiance

Written by author and minister Francis Bellamy, the Pledge of Allegiance was first published in *The Youth's Companion*, distributed across the country by the National Public Schools Celebration of Columbus Day, on September 8, 1892. "Bellamy had hoped that the pledge would be used by citizens in any country," according to an article on the USHistory.org website. The words were accompanied by the "Bellamy Salute," in which the right hand rested on the heart before being extended, palm down, toward the flag during recitation of the pledge. This gesture later caused some concern when it was said to resemble Hitler's salute.

Some words in the Pledge of Allegiance were replaced before it received official congressional approval and inclusion in the US Flag Code on June 22, 1942. "I pledge allegiance to my Flag and the Republic for which it stands, one nation, indivisible, with liberty and justice for all" was changed to "I pledge allegiance to the Flag of the United States of America and to the Republic for which it stands, one nation, indivisible, with liberty and justice for all" in 1923. The last change came in 1954 when the words "under God" were added after "one nation."

Created between 1941 and 1943, this poster promoted patriotism by reminding citizens to keep a tight lip about war communications.

The US Flag Code, designed to give guidance to civilians for displaying and caring for the flag (sometimes called the "national colors") was adopted on June 14, 1923, by a National Flag Conference represented by officials from the Army, Navy, and sixty-six other groups. Nineteen years later, in 1942, Congress passed a joint resolution that became Public Law 829, which gave exact rules for handling and displaying the flag. The Flag Code's basic premise is that "no disrespect should be shown to the flag of the United States of America."

Periodically, Congress issues a pamphlet on the proper care and use of the American flag. The following instructions are

"As I say the pledge and salute the flag, I feel the pride and gratitude that comes with having the blessing of living in this great country. I also feel the concern that comes with knowing that uncertainty lies ahead. We have survived many battles, many national and even global crises in our history, and we still have the liberty of living in the greatest country on this Earth. Can we continue to have the strength and unity of effort to meet that next challenge? Can I ensure my children and grandchildren and future generations have that same blessing? These are things that run through my mind. Bottom line, we should never take our flag and what it stands for, for granted."

—Adm. (Ret.) Mary Landry, USCG, Massachusetts

On the first morning of the new year in 2007, sailors assigned to the morning color detail aboard the submarine tender USS *Frank Cable* (AS 40) salute the holiday ensign. The flag is being flown at half-mast to honor the former president and Navy veteran Gerald R. Ford, who passed away on December 26, 2006. *(Photo credit: US Navy Mass Communications Specialist First Class Jeremy Johnson)*

courtesy of the manual entitled *Our Flag*, printed by the authority of House Concurrent Resolution 139, 108th Congress, US Government Printing Office, Washington, D.C., 2003.

Honoring the Flag

No disrespect should be shown to the flag of the United States of America; the flag should not be dipped to any person or thing. Regimental colors, state flags, and organization or institutional flags are to be dipped as a mark of honor.

(a) The flag should never be displayed with the union down, except as a signal of dire distress in instances of extreme danger to life or property.

(b) The flag should never touch anything beneath it, such as the ground, the floor, water, or merchandise.

(c) The flag should never be carried flat or horizontally, but always aloft and free.

(d) The flag should never be used as wearing apparel, bedding, or drapery. It should never be festooned, drawn back, nor up, in folds, but always allowed to fall free. Bunting of blue, white, and red, always arranged with the blue above, the white in the middle, and the red below, should be used for covering a speaker's desk, draping the front of the platform, and for decoration in general.

(e) The flag should never be fastened, displayed, used, or stored in such a manner as to permit it to be easily torn, soiled, or damaged in any way.

At sea, Coast Guard Seaman Apprentice James Wallace prepares to lower the national ensign in 2006 during evening colors on board the Coast Guard Cutter *Harriet Lane*. Colors is a traditional ceremony that takes place on board all US military vessels and bases every day at sunrise and sunset. *(Photo credit: US Coast Guard Kip Wadlow)*

(f) The flag should never be used as a covering for a ceiling.

(g) The flag should never have placed upon it, nor on any part of it, nor attached to it any mark, insignia, letter, word, figure, design, picture, or drawing of any nature.

(h) The flag should never be used as a receptacle for receiving, holding, carrying, or delivering anything.

(i) The flag should never be used for advertising purposes in any manner whatsoever. It should not be embroidered on such articles as cushions or handkerchiefs and the like, printed or otherwise impressed on paper napkins or boxes or anything that is designed for temporary use and discard. Advertising signs should not be fastened to a staff or halyard from which the flag is flown.

(j) No part of the flag should ever be used as a costume or athletic uniform. However, a flag patch may be affixed to the uniform of military personnel, firemen, policemen, and members of patriotic organizations. The flag represents a living country and is itself considered a living thing. Therefore, the lapel flag pin being a replica, should be worn on the left lapel near the heart.

(k) The flag, when it is in such condition that it is no longer a fitting emblem for display, should be destroyed in a dignified way, preferably by burning.

Displaying the Flag

(a) It is the universal custom to display the flag only from sunrise to sunset on buildings and on stationary flagstaffs in the open. However, when a patriotic effect is desired, the flag may be displayed twenty-four hours a day if properly illuminated during the hours of darkness.

(b) The flag should be hoisted briskly and lowered ceremoniously.

(c) The flag should not be displayed on days when the weather is inclement, except when an all weather flag is displayed.

(d) The flag should be displayed on all days, especially on:

HOLIDAY	DATE
New Year's Day	January 1
Inauguration Day	January 20
Lincoln's Birthday	February 12
Washington's Birthday	third Monday in February
Easter Sunday	(variable)
Mother's Day	second Sunday in May
Armed Forces Day	third Saturday in May
Memorial Day (half-staff until noon)	the last Monday in May
Flag Day	June 14
Independence Day	July 4
Labor Day	first Monday in September
Constitution Day	September 17
Columbus Day	second Monday in October
Navy Day	October 27
Veterans Day	November 11
Thanksgiving Day	fourth Thursday in November
Christmas Day	December 25;

As the last sliver of sunlight gent dips below the horizon in Kitter Maine, firefighter Michael Capa stands waiting for the call to low the colors aboard the CGC *Cam* The *Campbell*'s crew had returne its homeport just hours prior. It been on a counternarcotics patro in the Caribbean Sea, in which t crew seized more than ten thous pounds of cocaine. *(USCG photo by I Affairs Specialist Third Class Luke Pinneo)*

and such other days as may be proclaimed by the President of the United States; the birthdays of States (date of admission); and on State holidays.**

(e) The flag should be displayed daily on or near the main administration building of every public institution.

(f) The flag should be displayed in or near every polling place on election days.

(g) The flag should be displayed during school days in or near every schoolhouse.

** The flag is also flown on September 11.

Bluewater Elementary School students in Niceville, Florida, work together to fold the flag. Each morning and afternoon, students are responsible for raising and lowering the flag in front of the school. Featured from left to right: Maggie Babin, John Kotite, Emmaline Moye, and her sister Brianna. *(Photo credit: Amy Moye)*

Folding the Flag

1. Two persons, facing each other, hold the flag waist high and horizontally between them.
2. The lower striped section is folded, lengthwise, over the blue field. Hold bottom to top and edges together securely.
3. Fold the flag again, lengthwise, folded edge to open edge.
4. A triangular fold is started along the length of the flag, from the end to the heading by bringing the striped corner of the folded edge to meet the open edge.
5. The outer point is turned inward parallel with the open edge, forming a second triangle.
6. Repeat the triangular folding until the entire length of the flag is folded.
7. When the flag is completely folded only the triangular blue field should be visible.

White-gloved members of the Coast Guard Ceremonial Honor Guard fold the American flag during a memorial service for Petty Officer Steven Duque in Fort Lauderdale, Florida, in 2006. The flag detail often slips three brass shell-casings into the folded flag before presenting the flag to the family. Each casing represents one volley during the 21-gun salute. Petty Officer Duque died on August 17, 2006, in the line of duty while diving in the Arctic Ocean five hundred miles north of Barrow, Alaska. *(Photo credit: US Coast Guard Dana Warr)*

"Our flag's journey has been long. It has seen our nation through war and peace, triumph and tragedy. It flew above the walls of Fort Sumter, South Carolina, at the outset of the Civil War. It stood on Mount Suribachi on the island of Iwo Jima during World War II. During the civil rights movement, determined protesters on the streets of Selma, Alabama, proudly displayed its colors. Following the attacks of September 11, 2001, Old Glory flew over the southwestern wall of the Pentagon and the rubble of the World Trade Center. The Stars and Stripes tells our nation's story and embodies its highest ideals. Its display reminds us of America's promise and guides us toward a brighter tomorrow." **—President Barack Obama, June 14, 2009**

Honoring Those Who Served

The flag is placed so the union blue is at the head and over the left shoulder of the body. Do not lower the flag into the grave. After taps is played, the flag is folded into the symbolic tricornered shape.

After the flag is completely folded and tucked in, it takes on the appearance of a cocked hat, ever reminding us of the soldiers who served under Gen. George Washington and the sailors and marines who served under Capt. John Paul Jones, who were followed by their comrades and shipmates in the armed forces of the United States, preserving for us the rights, privileges, and freedoms we enjoy today.

The flag is generally presented to the appropriate family member after taps is played.

Stand facing the flag recipient and hold the folded flag waist high, with the straight edge facing the recipient. Lean toward the flag recipient and solemnly present the flag to the recipient.

At retirement ceremonies no taps is played, and the flag is ceremoniously presented, while Howard Schnauber's poem is read, celebrating and honoring those who served and are now retiring.

The Fort Carson Mounted Color Guard bears the national colors, marching in formation at the forefront of members of the National Cavalry Association, at the Fort Robinson State Park Parade Field, Nebraska, on January 11, 2010.
(US Army Photo by Pfc. Andrew Ingram)

Tomb of the Unknowns

Near the center of Arlington National Cemetery, in Arlington, Virginia, is a monument resting on top of the graves of unknown soldiers interred from World Wars I and II, the Korean War, and the Vietnam War. Called the Tomb of the Unknowns, it stands atop a hill overlooking Washington, D.C. On the marble panel facing Washington are the figures of VALOR, VICTORY, AND PEACE while the words HERE RESTS IN HONORED GLORY AN AMERICAN SOLDIER KNOWN BUT TO GOD are inscribed on the panel facing the plaza. The tomb is guarded every day of the year in every kind of weather, by members of the Third United States Infantry Regiment, called "The Old Guard." The regiment, according to its homepage, is "the oldest active-duty infantry unit in the Army, serving our nation since 1784." Since World War II, the Old Guard has been the official escort to the president. Soldiers considering the honor of serving as a sentinel at the tomb must pass several inspections and tests, including the

The epitaph of the Tomb of the Unknowns reads: HERE RESTS IN HONORED GLORY AN AMERICAN SOLDIER KNOWN BUT TO GOD

(Photo credit: Arlington National Cemetery)

manual of arms, history, uniform preparations, and guard-change ceremonies to earn the privilege of becoming an Old Guard member. These volunteer applicants must also have an unblemished military record.

The annual "flags in" tradition begins prior to Memorial Day weekend. The Old Guard places American flags before more than "260,000 gravestones and about 7,300 niches at the cemetery's columbarium" in under three hours, according to the cemetery's website. "Another 13,500 flags are placed at the Soldier's and Airmen's National Cemetery" in Washington, D.C., and American flags are also placed at the Tomb of the Unknowns. Before the cemetery reopens after the weekend, the flags are removed.

BIBLIOGRAPHY

Armed Forces Day copy accessed at www.defense.gov/afd/military/history.html on
   September 11, 2011.

Bering Sea accessed at www.uscg.mil/history/articles/BeringSea.asp on September 12,
   2011.

Blue Angels copy accessed at www.blueangels.navy.mil/team/ on September 11, 2011.

Fischer, David Hackett. *Washington's Crossing.* New York: Oxford University Press, 2004.

Flag copy accessed at http://americanhistory.si.edu/exhibitions/exhibition.
   cfm?key=38&exkey=70

Flag copy accessed at http://americanhistory.si.edu/starspangledbanner/faqs.aspx on
   September 11, 2011.

Flag copy accessed at http://americanhistory.si.edu/starspangledbanner/making-the-flag
   .aspx on September 11, 2011.

Flag copy accessed at http://gwpapers.virginia.edu/project/faq/govern.html on
   September 11, 2011.

Flag copy accessed at www.benningtonmuseum.org/flag.html on September 11, 2011.

Flag copy accessed at www.firstamendmentcenter.com/speech/flagburning/faqs.
   aspx?id=616&#q616

Flag copy accessed at www.flaglore.com/ on September 11, 2011.

Flag copy accessed at www.foundingfathers.info/stories/gadsden.html#franklin and www
   .interesting.com/stories/gadsden/ on September 11, 2011.

Flag copy accessed at www.newyorkled.com/nyc_events_Fleet_Week.htm on September
   11, 2011.

Flag photos and copy accessed at The Rare Flags Collection of Heather and Anthony
   Iasso, www.rareflags.com on September 11, 2011.

Four Freedoms copy accessed at www.ourdocuments.gov/doc.php?flash=true&doc=70 on
   September 12, 2011.

Gettysburg Address copy accessed at www.ourdocuments.gov/doc.php?flash=true&doc=36
   on September 12, 2011.

Haiti accessed at http://earthquake.usgs.gov/earthquakes/recenteqsww/Quakes/
   us2010rja6.php#details and http://earthquake.usgs.gov/earthquakes/recenteqsww/
   Quakes/us2010rja6.php#summary on September 12, 2011.

Hamilton, Schuyler. *History of the National Flag of the United States.* Philadelphia, PA: Lippincott, Gramba & C, 1853.

Historical Statistics of the United States: Colonial Times to 1970 accessed www.census.gov/prod/www/abs/statab.html on September 11, 2011.

Hurricane Katrina accessed at www.katrina.noaa.gov/ on September 12, 2011.

John Adams copy accessed at www.usa.gov/Topics/Independence_Day.shtml on September 11, 2011.

Memorial Day copy accessed at www.va.gov/opa/speceven/memday/history.asp on September 11, 2011.

National Flag Day copy accessed at www.nationalflagday.com/history.asp on September 12, 2011.

New York Times. "Red Sox Beat Cubs in Initial Game of World's Series Title," September 6, 1918, p. 14.

Pledge of Allegiance copy accessed at www.ushistory.org/documents/pledge.htm on September 12, 2011.

Preble, George Henry. *History of the Flag of the United States of America.* Boston, MA: A. Williams and Company, 1880.

President Lincoln copy accessed at http://showcase.netins.net/web/creative/lincoln/speeches/gettysburg.htm on September 12, 2011.

Quaife, Milo Milton; Weig, Melvin J; Appleman, Roy Edgar. *History of the United States Flag.* New York: Harpercollins, 1976.

Rodrigue copy accessed at www.wendyrodrigue.com/2010/09/god-bless-america-silkscreen-following.html on September 12, 2011. For more information, please visit www.National911Flag.org.

United States Congress, *Our Flag.* Printed by authority of House Concurrent Resolution 139, 108th Congress, U.S. Government Printing Office, Washington: 2003. accessed at www.senate.gov/reference/resources/pdf/ourflag.pdf, on September 11, 2011.

Vietnam War copy accessed at www.digitalhistory.uh.edu/modules/vietnam/index.cfm on September 12, 2011.

Winston Churchill copy accessed at www.guardian.co.uk/theguardian/2007/apr/20/greatspeeches1 on September 12, 2011.

Woodrow Wilson copy accessed at www.whitehouse.gov/about/presidents/woodrowwilson on September 12, 2011.

ABOUT THE AUTHORS

Martha LaGuardia-Kotite, a graduate of the Coast Guard Academy and a reserve officer, is the author of the four-time award-winning book, *So Others May Live* (with a foreword by Homeland Security Secretary Tom Ridge). Recently, she served as then Commandant Admiral Thad W. Allen's press secretary during the Haiti earthquake and during his role as the National Incident Commander for the Deepwater Horizon Oil Spill. She is a member of the National Press Club and the Authors Guild.

Trish Marx writes nonfiction books for children in kindergarten through twelfth grade. Her assignments have taken her to China, Peru, Israel, Kosovo, and recently the Middle East. Her books have received awards and recognition such as Notable Books in the area of Social Studies, Parents' Choice, Booklinks Best 10 Books of the Year list, and a 2011 Sydney Taylor Notable Book for Older Readers. She is a member of PEN, the Authors Guild, and the National Press Club.